The Sikh Com
of Manchester

Sarup Singh Landa
UK

Copy rights reserved by;-
Sarup Singh Landa Manchester UK
Ravinder Singh Landa Manchester UK
Permjit Singh Landa Manchester UK

First Published; - 2023
ISBN 978-1-915025-98-2

Typeset and edited by Beacon Publishing Services
www.beaconbooks.net/bps

Pardesi Books
Manchester UK

The Sikh Community of Manchester

A Personal Perspective

By
Sarup Singh Landa

Dedicated to
Grandfather Pandit Nanak Singh Ji Garhi
Village Garhi Dist Udhampur
Jammu & Kashmir

And
Father Gyani Mehar Singh Pardesi
First Sikh High Priest of Guru Nanak Nirankari Gurdwara
Managed by Sewak Jatha of Manchester
Monton Street Moss Side
Manchester UK

Contents

Acknowledgements

To take on such enormous task of gathering information about the community was not, and has not been straight forward. It was very searching and hard work and a very steep cliff to climb. It needed much encouragement and a hard push to start the climb, and that encouragement came from my colleague and a dear friend Anuj Rampal, who encouraged me to take a very deep breath and start the climb. He himself knew that I have never put pen to paper in all my years but nevertheless pushed me into the deep end of the writing pool. Also I am grateful to members of all five Gurdwara's of Manchester with whom I have been connected for so many decades. The names mentioned are of our past elders most of whom have departed—my respects to them and their families. I felt it necessary to mention their names so that their siblings can be proud of them. I profoundly apologise in advance if anyone feels otherwise

I am grateful to my grandfather in whose lap I sat as youngster while he recited the Sikh scriptures in my home town of Garhi. Also to my uncle Giani sunder Singh Sagar Ji, in Manchester who was my role model. He not only inspired me but also guided me in the right direction. I am thankful to him for letting me have his original dossier which he produced for the Manchester City Council Transport Committee about the British Sikh forces and how they sacrificed their lives for the British Empire in the battlefields still keeping their religion and faith intact during the struggles. It was published to make the Manchester City Transport Department aware about the religion and its ethics. In order to get Sikhs with turbans employed on the city buses. I am in debt and proud to re-write and include the original document which was a historic achievement for the Manchester Sikh community in achieving their goal of gaining employment as bus drivers and conductors without losing their religious ethnicity.

My profound thanks go to Sardar Surjit Singh Bhaker, and Sardar Dharmbir Singh Landa for making available to me an original copy of the fund collection list of 1952, without which I could not have envisaged to begin writing this short history. Sincere thanks also to Parkash Singh Potiwal and Gurteak Singh Swaley for their valuable suggestions and Sardar Kuldip Singh Sira for his valuable insight into the Sikh Association history and its origins. To Sardar Pritam Singh Rasila, for his valuable time with whom I had lengthy discourses and gave me valuable insight to the past history of Hulme Gurdwara Sahib. My thanks also goes to Luckveer Singh for helpful suggestions. I am in gratitude to my friend Sardar Baldev Singh Jugdy for his support in publication of this book, and my profound thanks to all my friends who from time to time kept encouraging me to complete this project. Above all, my gratitude and respects goes to those elders mentioned in this short history. Without their determination and hard work, we the Manchester Sikhs whether Bhatra Sikh or Jaat Sikhs of Manchester wouldn't be where we are today

foreword

Some people dream about writing a book or memoir based on their lives and achievements. For most it just remains a dream. This book is not a dream but actual events which took place and witnessed by the author who lived through them. And with the community and Guru's blessings the author has put pen to paper and tried to present history as it happened in the early 1960s and 1980s while residing in Manchester for the last 6 decades.

He has recorded events as it happened over the last 60 years. With his vast knowledge of the Manchester Sikh community and its origins, the author has written this history of the past seventy years in great detail and has tried to present the facts of the Sikhs in the early years and what they faced when they arrived.

His whole life and career has been dedicated to the Sikh community. With grace and blessings he developed the vision of this book *The Sikh Community of Manchester: from a personal perspective.*

This book is a testament to the community from where the author gained spiritual knowledge and societal strength. I would like to take this opportunity to wish the author every success with the book which has been a labour of love.

Anuj Rampal
Author, Digital Marketer
Manchester, UK 2023

Preface

The global society is passing through a very crucial phase in its history. Basic characteristics of our hallowed values are on the verge of crumbling. The impact of mass media, TV, mobile phones, and the internet has now taken over our lives. We find it hard to keep pace with life in the fast lane.

We, the Sikhs, came to this country in search of a better life, in a new country, without any knowledge of its language or European lifestyles. Nevertheless, having the British rule India for over two hundred years had given us somewhat of a head start in how to tackle the difficulties ahead, and no doubt they faced hostilities in the early years. Nevertheless, having a very strong and sound religious heritage, particularly the Bhatra Sangat, was very strict in keeping their faith intact. To see how they achieved this through hostile times when discrimination was ubiquitous, we have to look back in history. But nevertheless, they toiled through hardship to make ends meet. We need to praise our elders, the high values of our religion, and the proud heritage we have inherited from them.

To keep that inheritance intact, one needs to keep a record of our past history, of our predecessors and their achievements. Therefore, it becomes essential to document the past so that the reader can immerse themselves in the thoughts of their past. To revive the history of the last 70-80 years, although there is very little documented evidence available, but whatever is available should be kept safe. Therefore, it would take a very determined individual to take on the enormous task of putting pen to paper and threading together pieces of history of the Sikh community in Manchester.

I came to England in 1959 at a very young age, and everything I have witnessed and understood, I have tried to write in this short history.

It is important to have records of the past that future generations can refer to. If anyone were to contest our history, then it would be useful to have written evidence to challenge it. History has to be written so that future generations can refer to their past and feel connected. By being aware of their peers' accomplishments and preserving their uniqueness, their legacy can be remembered forever.

History has its roots in the past, which has to be documented from time to time. If that's not done, then communities can lose their heritage in many ways. One must remember that times are changing now, and with that, the thoughts, ideals, and of course, the minds are guided by mass media, which now plays a very large part in our lives. In the earlier years, the influence of the media was very minimal, and television would broadcast only up till 11 pm, after which the national anthem would play. Modern technology has developed so rapidly that everything is now available all the time, including terrestrial television.

In the modern era, it has become more important to document our past that our predecessors, who toiled to leave a rich heritage during hostile times. They should be remembered by their offspring and future generations. This little effort is a small venture to document from my memory what I have lived through, seen, and experienced firsthand as it happened.

Writing this short history of the Manchester Sikh community is my personal account and testimony of which I have experienced living in the community for the last seven decades in Manchester. In that time, I have seen and witnessed so many changes, and many important events have taken place. I have witnessed many things firsthand, but unfortunately, little has been documented about these changes when they took place. Nevertheless, our elders at the time felt it necessary to propagate their faith and community, even as they faced so many difficult hurdles on the way in the early years. They never lost confidence in their ways, and they became an integral part of the host

Sarup Singh Landa
Manchester UK 2023

Sikh Religion

The foundation of the Sikh religion was laid by Guru Nanak Dev Ji, who was born in 1469 at Talwandi Rai Bhoe, now known as Nankana Sahib in Pakistan. His father, Kalyan Chand, belonged to the Bedi clan of the Kshatriyas. Guru Nanak grew up in his ancestral village and those early years are described in the Janamsakhis.

Guru Nanak believed in all humanity and one God, and said that all people are equal and there is no Hindu or Muslim. God made everything in the world. God being present in everyone and all things, and we should worship no other than God. He encouraged the name of God, preached equality between people, tried to remove the caste system between people, which was very prevalent at the time. All people are children of God.

In order to preach, Guru Nanak Dev Ji took on arduous journeys, taking along with him his two companions, Bhai Mardana, a Muslim, and Bhai Bala, a Hindu. On their journeys, Guru Nanak Dev Ji along with his companions visited many different places of worship, preaching the name of one God. In 1510, Guru Nanak Dev Ji undertook a second religious tour and visited Sri Lanka, then known as Sangladeep. (Ceylon).

A meeting took place between Raja Shivnabh, grandfather of Changa Rai, whose followers were all academic; but the country had seven different divisions in their kingdom, which Guru Nanak Dev Ji united together and made Changa Rai their leader. Baba Changa Rai became a disciple of Guru Nanak Dev Ji and earned the title of Changa Bhatt. And Guru Ji bestowed his followers with the name of Sangat. The word Bhat, according to the Sikh encyclopedia, Bhat, is related to Sanskrit and the word Bhatta, signifying a bard or a poet. Also mentioned in the "Janamsakhis", a group led by Baba Changa Rai is described in a very old document called "Haqiqat Rah Mukam". The Sikh encyclopedia discusses this link between them and Bhat Sikhs.

It is stated in the Gur Shabad Ratnakar Mahankhosh that the Bhatts who's Gurbani is incorporated in the Guru Granth Sahib Ji, were bards (poets) of Guru Darbar who met Guru Nanak Dev Ji in Sangladeep (Ceylon) in 1510.

It was during Guru Nanak's visit to Ceylon that he composed the Pransangali, which contained an account of the silent palace of God, the manner of meditating on Him, the private utterance of the Guru, and the nature of the soul and body. Following are the opening verses:

The supreme state is altogether a void;
All people say:
In the supreme state there is no rejoicing or mourning;
In the supreme state there are felt no hopes or desire;
In the supreme state are seen no casts or cast-marks;
In the supreme state are no sermons or singing of hymns;
In the supreme state abideth heavenly meditation;
In the supreme state are those who know themselves.
Nanak, my mind is satisfied with the supreme state.

This is the meeting that took place between Guru Nanak and Raja Shivnabh, the grandfather of Changa Rai.

It is also mentioned in the Encyclopaedia of Sikh Religion and Culture by Ramesh Chander Dogra and Dr. Gobind Singh Mansukhani, that Bhatra was a peddler who was of Brahmin origin from Madho Mal, a Brahmin Rishi, a singer and poet. He married Kam Kundla and from then descended the Madhwas or Bhatra's. Madho was born and died in Ceylon (Sri Lanka), where a Sikh Temple known as Dera Baba was built. Bhats were bards of the Gurus Darbar who wrote the Bhatt-Vahis (volumes) which were brought to public notice by Gyani Gurdit Singh, who discovered genealogy material from Bhai Sant Singh, resident of village Jind district Karnal. In 1961, following this, he also published an article in the journal 'Alochna'. Later in 1974, Professor Fauja Singh referred to the "Bhat–Vahis" in his article "Guru Tegh Bhadur". Professor Sahib Singh Ji also refers to the article by Gyani Gurdit Singh in the preface of his book "Bhatta-De-Sawaye."

After Professor Fauja Singh's article, the "Bhat–Vahis" are now being researched in the Punjabi university of Patiala and various other universities across India. In the 14th and 15th centuries, each village or group had their own family priests who used to oversee their religious needs, and they recorded their patron's important events so as to creating a family tree. In return, they used to receive alms of gifts and some monetary help. They usually lived near the pilgrim centres and were experts in reading palmistry, which they inherited from their forefathers, all of them from Brahmins cast.

A very old document named "Haqiqat-Rah-Mukam" describes the meeting of Guru Nanak with Raja Shivnabh (p1248) along with an 18th century hand written copy of Bir Bhai Bannu which mentions the start of Bhat Sikh Sangat. In the Janamsakhis, it is mentioned how the grandson of Raja Shivnabh had earned the title of Bhat-Rai, the Raja of poets. Then he settled himself and his followers all over India as missionaries to spread the word of Guru Nanak, where many northern Indians became Bhat Sikhs. The majority were from Brahmin cast (Bhat-Clan) as Baba Changa shared the Brahmin heritage. The Sangat had many members from different areas of the Sikh caste spectrum, such as Hindu, Rajputs, Jats who joined the Bhat Sikh missionary efforts.

The Bhats also contributed 123 compositions in the Sri Guru Granth Sahib (pp. 1389-1409), known as "Bhata de Savaiyye". Their hereditary occupations consisted of bard, poets, missionaries, astrologers, genealogists, and salesman.

Sardar Mewa Singh Garhi, in his book the second Udasis, of Guru Nanak and Guru Ki Sangat he refers to a book by Baba Changa Rai, who describes the second missionary tour (Udasis) of Guru Nanak in 1510 which he refers to an article by M.S. Ahluwalia a senior fellow historical researcher. He offers evidence of Guru Nanak's presences in Sangladeep (Sri Lanka) in which he details the journey of Baba Changa Rai and his followers who also became disciples Guru Ji, and later followed in search of Guru Ji to which most of them settled down in south India. Groups of them had gone in different directions in search of Guru Ji which meant that they may have also settled in different parts of India.

Author H.A Rose in his book, states that the Sikh Sangat set-up by Guru Ji, had followed him into India. However, being in search for so many years, by the time they met up with Guru Ji it was the time of fourth Guru Ramdas Ji. As they were bards and wrote prayers in honour of Guru Ji which they sang each day.

Latter the fifth Guru, Guru Arjan Dev Ji compiled the Adi-Granth Sahib at Ramsar sarowar, Guru also included "Bhatta-Dy-Sawaye" which are now recited each morning during Parkash of Guru Granth Sahib in Harimander Sahib Amritsar.

It is stated in the University of Derby's multi-Faith network directory of religions in the UK that the first Sikh to settle in England was

Duleep Singh, son of Maharaja Ranjit Singh, who arrived in Norfolk at Elveden Estate in 1854.

After the British annexed India through the East India Company and ruled the subcontinent for many years, many Sikhs were enlisted in the British Indian army in the 1920s. The late Gyani Rattan Singh Shaad states in his book Krantik Lehra that the first Bhatra Sikhs to set foot on British soil in 1924 were:

* Sardar Hakam Singh Dauu from Glotian Kalan (Pakistan)
* His son, Hari Singh Raja
* Sardar Nihal Singh
* Sardar Veer Singh Gorkha
* Sardar Peshora Singh Gola
* His son Sardar Gushal Singh

The Author

I, myself, came to England at a young age. My father was a Sikh priest at Gurdwara Sahib in Manchester. Although most of my schooling was done back home in Udhampur, Jammu and Kashmir, I only attended school in Manchester for a short period. My knowledge of English was very minimal by the time I left school at sixteen, so I had to attend night classes to improve my understanding of the English language.

After leaving school, I began my working life in a small factory for a short period. From there, I changed my job and started working in a cotton mill in Oldham town. I worked the night shift in the ring spinning room, and this became a set pattern for the rest of my life. However, I was determined to continue learning and started working in different departments of the cotton industry. This allowed me to gain knowledge of various aspects of the cotton mills, including ring spinning, doubling, carding, weaving, and other processes related to woven cloth.

In the 1970s, many of my colleagues found employment in the transport industries, and I also desired a change. I applied for a bus conductor vacancy at Manchester Corporation Transport Department and became a bus conductor driver. This career change lasted for the next twenty-six years until the transport system was deregulated in 1986 by the Conservative government. Afterward, I started working in a freight company for the next fifteen years. However, the company underwent drastic changes, and I was eventually made redundant and retired at the age of 69.

Throughout my life, I have remained a devoted Sikh, and being the sibling of a former Sikh priest, I was offered the job of Sikh priest for a short period. However, the Sikh Temple eventually began employing priests from abroad. I have been an active member of the Sikh community in Manchester and have served in various roles in the city's Gurdwaras, particularly in the capacity of a Sikh priest. My life as a practicing Sikh living within the Sikh communities has had a significant influence on my entire family, and for that, I am grateful to Guru Ji for his never-ending blessings.

Dharamsala-cum-Gurdwara London UK

During the British colonial Raj of India, many Indian subjects came to Britain to work and study. India, being a colony of the British Empire, its subjects travelled freely from India to Europe. One prominent Raja of Punjab, Maha Raja Bhupinder Singh, was a frequent visitor to his residence in London at Sinclair Road W14 0NJ. Many Punjabi and Indians of all religions lived in the nearby vicinity of the Dharamsala, after each visit the Maha Raja used to return to india and his premises were used as Dharamsala for his countrymen. After his return to India, the premises were used as a Dharamsala for his countrymen, where they could all meet. In 1908, a group of them formed a society named Khalsa Jatha of London. The society was only three years old when the Maha Raja came to London on his regular visit in 1911. Then he was approached by this group for permission to convert one of the rooms in the Dharamsala into a prayer room. The Maha Raja obliged them with the permission and donated £100 pounds towards the conversion. Once the Guru Granth Sahib was installed and regular prayers began to take place, people from all walks of life began to visit the premises. The majority of Sikhs living in London at that time were from the Bhatra caste, being the majority, they were leaders in forming the society and the first president elect was Gyani Rattan Singh Shaad.

In the back row of the photo standing is Sardar Udham Singh Shaheed, who also used to visit the Dharamsala regularly. Udham Singh, a freedom fighter, was constantly under surveillance of the British Indian authorities. He made his way to England in 1934, evading the British Indian police authorities.

Udham Singh Azad – alias "Ram Mohamed Singh Azad"

In 1934, Sardar Udham Singh Azad, alias "Ram Mohamed Singh Azad", a freedom fighter influenced by his adversary Shaheed Bhagat Singh, had made his way to Britain to take revenge of the Amritsar Massacre. A massacre which took place on 13th April 1919 at Jalianwala Bagh under the leadership of British army officer General Michael O'Dwyer, who ordered his troops to open fire on unarmed innocent people who had gathered for a rally, in which many men, women and children were slaughtered by his troops. Udham Singh, a young man of only twenty years of age, already a freedom fighter, saw this massacre at first hand, in which his family members were massacred; there and then he vowed to take revenge. Because all the freedom fighters were under the surveillance of the authorities and were in and out of jails, to avoid this he migrated to the United States in 1924, where he joined the American Ghadar Party "revolutionary party of America", and became an active member of the party. After a short time, he was recalled to India by his adversary. It was impossible to return to India with the same name, therefore, he changed his name to "Ram Mohamed Singh Azad", and returned to India with twenty-five colleagues, bringing with them ammunition and guns from America.

No sooner had he arrived in India, he was arrested and jailed for five years. After his release in 1931, evading police, he made his way to Kashmir, and from there to Germany, and from there he came to London in 1934 and took residence in an Italian cafe in the city of Bedford with his companion Bakhtavar Singh. Both of them met with Gyani Rattan Singh Shaad in Nov/Dec 1938 and became friends and started to visit the Dharamsala. Gyani Ji wrote Krantik "revolutionary" poems for him. After twenty-one years of waiting, his wish began to bear fruit, although he had become friends with everyone, he never revealed his intentions to anyone. On 13th March 1940, the East India Association and Royal Central Society of London held a function at Caxton Hall and General Michael O'Dwyer as their guest speaker, which was well advertised locally and Udham Singh's opportunity arose, and he decided to attend the function, concealing a revolver, he entered Caxton Hall. During his speech, Michael O'Dwyer stated these words "If it was up to me I would have Massacred the whole town of Amritsar", as he was speaking these words, Ram Mohamed Singh Azad shot dead Michael O'Dwyer and fulfilled his twenty-one year vow which he took on 13th April 1919.

The people injured in the shooting were Louis Dane, Lawrence Dundas and Charles Cochrane Baillie. There being no other casualties, he was immediately arrested and charged with the murder of Michael O'Dwyer. The incident was well published by the media and all the London resident Asians gathered on 19th March at Commercial Road London and formed a committee to collect funds for a defence solicitor. Members of the defence committee were: Sri Krishan Mennon – Chair of Indian league as general secretary; Dr Diwan Singh Ji as advisor; Sardar Shiv Singh Ji Birmingham cashier – Khalsa Jatha gen secretary; Mr. Akbar Khan B.A.LLB Convener; Sardar Sant Singh Pardesi; Mr. Noor Din Qureshi; G. Rattan Singh Shaad; Mr. Din Mohamed; Sardar Didar Singh; Sardar Ravel Singh – support agent.

A fund of £1650 was collected and a donation came from the American Ghadar Party. Ram Mohamed Singh Azad was formally charged with the murder of Michael O'Dwyer on 1st April 1940 and was sent to Brixton prison awaiting his trial. While awaiting his trial at Brixton prison, Mr. Singh went on a hunger strike for 42 days and was force-fed by the prison staff.

His trial began on 4th June 1940 at Central Criminal Court Old Bailey, before Justice Atkinson and V.K. Krishna Mennon and St. John Hutchinson representing him. When the Judge asked Udham Singh about his motivation, Singh explained; "I did it because I had a grudge against him, he deserved it, and he was the real culprit who wanted to crush the spirit of my people, so I have crushed him! For the last twenty-one years, I have been trying to wreak vengeance and now I am happy that I have done the job. I am not scared of death. I am dying for my country. I have seen people starving in my country under the British rule. I have always protested against this because I felt that it was my duty. There is no greater honour that can be bestowed on me than dying for my motherland." Udham Singh Shaheed, alias Ram Mohamed Singh Azad, was convicted of murder and sentenced to death on 31st July 1940. He was hanged at Pentonville Prison, Caledonian Road, Barnsbury, London N17.

In 1974, the remains of Shaheed Udham Singh were exhumed and repatriated to India, by the request of MLA Sadhu Singh Thind, and he accompanied the remains back to India, where the casket was received by the Indian prime minister. Later, his remains were cremated at his birthplace Sunam in Punjab and his ashes scattered in the river Sutlej and part of his ashes are kept in a sealed urn at Jalianwala Bagh Amritsar.

Ek-Onkar Sat Guru Prasad

The full list of funds collected for the Gurdwara Sahib in 1952. with names and amounts donated [1]

Nanak Nirankari Gurdwara Manchester.

Manchester	£	Shillings
Mela Singh, Bhadur Singh, Hakam Singh Bhaker	10	0
Kazan Singh, Jeeva Singh, Ajit Singh, Lahore Waley	10	0
Bhil Singh Landa, Gehna Singh Landa	10	0
Sant Singh Pardesi, Bakunt Singh Digwa	10	0
Chiba Singh, Bakshi Singh, Gopal Singh Bhaker	10	0
Daulat Singh, Nihal Singh Potiwal	5	0
Balwant Singh, Diwan Singh, Gurpal Singh	5	0
Ram Singh, Mega Singh, Sawaran Singh Gozra	7	10
Inder Singh, Sital Singh, Bhadur Singh Laard	5	0
Lahorey Singh Berra, Mohan Singh Rador	5	0
Chanan Singh, Lahore Singh Berra Rador	2	10
Mohkam Singh, Jeet Singh, Chuni Singh Potiwal	6	5
Mela Singh, Nihal Singh Potiwal	5	5
Waryam Singh Tari, Nauria Singh Rador	7	10
Munshi Singh Sofi, Bhil Singh Landa	5	5
Pheru Singh, Pindya Singh, Esher Singh Landa	6	5
Jeet Singh, Mohan Singh, Daleep Singh Landa	5	0
Dayal Singh, Isher Singh Bhaker	3	10
Tunda Singh, Mehnga Singh Gozra	2	10
Joginder Singh, Sundar Singh Gola	2	10
Khazan Singh, Hari Singh Landa	2	0
Sagar Singh, Chuurr Singh Swaley	1	10
Phuman Singh, Diwan Singh Bhaker	1	5

1 The list is written in Punjabi, it has been translated in English for the benefit of the readers.

Gurbachan Singh, Inder Singh Rador	3	15
Jeet Singh, Jodha Singh Landa	2	10
Tirath Singh, Baag Singh Rador	5	0
Inder Singh Shashtry, Baag Singh Rador	5	0
Daleep Singh, Diwan Singh Digwa	3	0
Mehl Singh Pana Singh Landa	2	10
Barkat Singh, Heera Singh Sidh	2	10
Lahori Singh Kalnoria, Lachman Singh Rador	2	10
Tunda Singh, Kesar Singh Kasbia	2	10
Mohkam Singh, Pindya Singh Landa	2	10
Chuni Singh, Saram Singh Digwa	2	10
Prof Jagjit Singh, Hakam Singh	5	0
Jaswant Singh, Pirmal Singh Potiwal	1	5
Kulwant Singh, Narayan Singh Bhateja	11	0
Pandit Bindha Madhva Ganesh	2	10
Ajeet Singh, Phuman Singh Batuu	4	0
Babu Sudarshan Kumar, Lala Diwan Chand	1	0
Total	187	15

Liver pool 31/1/1954	£	Shillings
Gushal Singh, Pashora Singh, Gola	5.	0
Kamal Kishor Singh, Dakar Singh Bhese	5	5
Darshan Singh,, Fakir Singh Landa	5	5
Ujagar Singh, Ruldhu Singh, Banti Singh Roudh	7	10
Harbans Singh, Natha Singh, Jeet Singh Bhaker	5	0
Kundan Singh, Dayal Singh Digwa	2	10
Bhadur Singh Chand, Javhar Singh Chand Digwa	5	5
Harnam Singh, Kesar Singh Bhandhari Digwa	5	5
Hoshiar Singh, Pashora Singh Gola	3	15
Karta Singh, Jawahar Singh Digwa	2	10

Waryam Singh, Bari Singh, Piayar Singh Rador	3	15
Saudgar Singh, Swami Mohan Singh, Darshan Singh Roudh	9	10
Isher Singh, Lachan Singh Taak	2	10
Bhadur Singh, Ganda Singh Bhatti	2	10
Total	65	10

Leeds 2/2/1954	£	Shillings
Balwant Singh,Gurshal Singh, Akali Niranjan Singh Landa	10	10
Chuni Singh, Daulat Singh Digwa	2	10
Bhadur Singh, Ganda Singh, Mohkam Singh Landa	5	0
Babu Singh, Ganda Singh Landa	2	10
Tehel Singh, Buta Singh, Hajara Singh Rador	7	10
Joginder Singh, Mohkam Singh Laard	2	10
Ganga Singh, Mohkam Singh	7	10
Total	38	0

Newcastle 3/2/1954	£	Shillings
Shingar Singh, Lehna Singh, Harbans Singh Gola	10	0
Jarnail Singh ,Partab Singh Digwa	2	10
Changi Singh, Raam Singh Landa	3	10
Hakam Singh, Kirpal Singh, Teja Singh Digwa	5	0
Gurbachan sing, Sant Singh Roudh	2	10
Total	23	10

City of Carlisle 5-2-1954	£	Shillings
Sundar Singh Sagar &Pana Singh landa	1	0
Mehl Singh, Amar Singh, Jit Singh Roudh	10	0
Phuman Singh, Primal Singh Potiwal	5	0
Munshi Singh, Kalu Singh Digwa	2	10
Tehal Singh Dogar Singh Rador	2	10

Total	21	0

City of Nottingham 7-2-1954		
Amar Singh, Nihal Singh Rador	2	10
Nader Singh	10	0
Mule Singh, Vaisakhi Singh Landa	2	10
Kher Singh, Piara Singh, Sukhu Singh Potiwal	5	5
Gushal Singh, Kishan Singh Roudh	2	10
Avtar Singh, Veer Singh Rador	2	10
Joginder Singh, Parkash Singh Rador	2	10
Total	27	15

City of Birmingham 8-2-1954	£	Shillings
Buta Singh, Gobind Singh Landa	5	5
Kulwant Singh, Budu Singh Digwa	4	0
Mulakh Singh, Isher Singh Rador	2	10
Phuman Singh, Mohan Singh Rador	2	10
Makhan Singh, Banarsi Singh, Ladha Singh Bhaker	5	5
Darshan Singh, Mela Singh, Garib Singh Bhaker	5	5
Bhadur Singh, Sdavarti Singh Landa	2	10
Babau Singh, Fali Singh Digwa	2	10
Godhi Singh, Mohr Singh, Sown Singh Swali	10	0
Balwant Singh, Lachman Singh Swali	2	10
Nirjan Singh, Sunder Singh Swali	2	10
Lal Singh, Desa Singh, Baan Singh Bhaker	5	0
Tehal Singh, Desa Singh Bhaker	2	10
Niranjan Singh, Buta Singh Roudh	2	10
Bagwan Singh, Budhu Singh Digwa	2	10
Waryam Singh, Heera Singh, Santokh Singh Loha	3	15
Jagtar Singh, Harnam Singh Potiwal	5	5

Hajara Singh, Havela Singh Landa	2	10
Sr. Singh, Diwan Singh Rador	2	10
Sarup Singh, Raja Singh Rador	2	10
Bawa Singh Chuhaan	2	10
Tara Singh, Deru Singh Landa	2	10
Fauja Singh, Balwant Singh Rador	6	5
Maknda Singh, Bawa Singh, Raja Singh Potiwal	6	5
Parkash Singh, Nanak Singh Potiwal	2	10
Puran Singh, Mula Singh Rador	5	5
Chanan Singh, Bawa Mani Das Digwa	2	10
Total	£101	10

City of London 28-3-1954	£	Shillings
Darshan Singh, Mokham Singh Laard	5	0
Ujagar Singh, Jiwa Singh, Pritam Singh Bhaker Lahore wale Pardhan	5	0
Sant Singh, Kartar Singh, Makha Singh Bhaker	5	5
Darshan Singh, Tunda Singh Bhaker	5	5
Sawan Singh, Gobind Singh Bhaker	5	5
Inder Singh, Diwan Singh Potiwal	5	5
Puran Singh, Diwan Singh Potiwal	2	10
Hansa Singh, Gujar Singh Rador	5	0
Darshan Singh, Sadhu Singh, Shingar Singh Potiwal	5	5
Harbhajan Singh, name not readable	2	0
Sawaran Singh, Ram Singh Landa	5	0
Sawaran Singh, Gurcharan Singh, Gobind Singh Potiwal	5	5
Waryam Singh, Raja Singh Babau Taak	5	5
Shingar Singh, Buda Singh Taak	2	10
Sr. Singh, Nanak Singh, Harnam Singh Bhaker	5	5
Waryam Singh, Jinder Singh Landa	2	10
Inder Singh Dilber, Partab Singh Landa	5	5
Hari Singh Nalva, Miaa Singh Digwa	5	5

Bhadur Singh, Khesa Singh Landa	2	10
Bachiter Singh, Chiman Singh Bhaker (Jiva singh) Lahore wale	5	5
Khzan Singh, Jit Singh, Heera Singh Lohe	5	5
Hari Singh, Ganda Singh, Sr. Singh	5	5
Amar Singh, Mela Singh Rador	5	5
Desa Singh, Maknda Singh Kasbia	2	10
Shingar Singh, Ganda Singh Potiwal	2	10
Jaga Singh Goodman, Dasa Singh Swaley	2	10
Santokh Singh, Vaisakhi Singh Rador	3	0
Gehna Singh, Jeet Singh, Burr Singh Gola	5	0
Rattan Singh, Bhadur Singh, Gehna Singh Gola	5	0
Veer Singh, Mehar Singh Bhaker	2	10
Waryam Singh, Shaam Singh, Sohan Singh Rador	5	0
Sewa Singh, Veer Singh Digwa	2	10
Buta Singh, Kaka Singh Kasbia	5	5
Piara Singh, Madraji Singh Bhaker	2	10
Gian Singh, Heera Singh Loha	2	10
Puran Singh, Bailey Singh Swaley	2	10
Kher Singh, Ganda Singh Digwa	2	10
Mewa Singh, Kartar Singh Digwa	3	0
Chajjuu Singh, Hakam Singh Digwa	2	10
Sohan Singh Bola, Mehnga Singh Rador	2	10
Mansa Singh	1	0
Mehar Singh Tattoo, Mia Singh Digwa	1	10
Shingar Singh, Kesar Singh Laard	1	5
Mull Singh, Sant Singh Bhaker	1	0
Inder Singh, Khzan Singh	0	10
Mohkam Singh, Pindya Gola	0	10
Balwant Singh, Sant Singh Bhaker	1	0
Chanan Singh, not red able	3	0
Mehnga Singh, Baiey Singh Gujra	2	10

Inder Singh, Manak Singh Digwa	3	0
Jaswant Singh, ram Singh Digwa	4	0
Hansa Singh, Kesar Singh Laard	2	10
Fateh Singh, Master Tara Singh Ragi, Taak secretary	5	0
Joga Singh, Barkat Singh, Satnam Singh, Taak	2	10
Pritam Singh, Gian Singh Ragi Taak	2	10
Jit Singh, Vaisakhi Singh Swaley	2	10
Total	£201	10

	£	Shillings
Mohkam Singh, Pushkar Singh Bhaker	2	10
Jamir Singh, Inder Singh, Kesar Singh, Digwa Jathedar	5	0
Fakir Singh, Lal Singh Taak	1	5
Sr. Singh, Sant Chetan Das Digwa	10	0
Mehar Singh Pardesi Nanak Singh Landa	1	5
Total	20	0
Total amount collected	£685	7

Before decimalisation the currency in circulation known as the imperial system consisted of pounds, shilling and pence. Notes were in denominations of five pound one pound and ten shilling notes Coins in use were the farthing, the ha'penny, the penny, a threepenny bit, the sixpence (the tanner), the shilling (the bob), the 2 shilling coin and the half crown.

Guru Nanak Nirankari Gurdwara

Courtesy of Guru Nanak Nirankari Gurdwara
Monton Street Moss Side

Manchester Gurdwara history began in 1950. A devoted family held weekly Sunday services at their residence, in which everyone was invited to take part. At their residence in Moss Side, they were the only family in possession of the Guru Granth Sahib Ji. Being ardent devotees of the Sikh faith, they kept the ritual of holding prayer meetings alive in the community. As time passed, the number of families increased, the space got smaller, and the demands of the community also increased. It was then felt by the consensus that a larger premises should be found to facilitate the growing demands of the Sikh families.

In 1952/53, a decision was taken by the congregation to establish a Gurdwara Sahib and start a collection fund to finance the project. So that the religious and cultural demands of the Sikhs and their families could be taken care of, to spearhead the project a committee of four respected gentlemen was designated to oversee the collection funds. The four designated gentlemen were:

* Sardar Bhil Singh Landa
* Sardar Mela Singh Bhaker
* Sardar Sant Singh Pardesi
* Sardar Khazan Singh Bhaker

Group Photo Monton St Gurdwara Manchester 1954

The four respected missionaries embarked on a mission with Guru Ji's blessings. The four devoted missionaries travelled to all UK cities where Bhat Sikh Sangat was resident, collecting funds for the Gurdwara Sahib.

In the 1950s, the state of the country was not in any way very stable. The British had recently survived from the Second World War and were recuperating from it. The losses faced by the allied forces were phenomenal, and for that reason, the economy was very low. The other factor was that, Bhatra Sikhs were here to work and were single men. So what little they earned through door-to-door sales they endeavored to send back to their families. Nevertheless, they donated whatever little they could and were very eager to do so. Large or small amounts, but made sure they donated. Their names, towns, and amounts were noted, and once the Gurdwara Sahib was established, the full list with their names, towns, and amounts took pride of place in the main prayer hall of the Gurdwara Sahib.

The concerted effort of the four respected gentlemen, who were elders of the community, travelled through cold weather without any thought of illness. This was their ingrained devotion of their religion and faith in their beliefs which led them through thick and thin, offering their abnegating services to the community. Not only that, but went above and beyond to fulfill their mission which the Sangat has bestowed on them.

Master Tara Singh Chief Minister of Punjab Visits Manchester's First Gurdwara 1954

The mission started in 1952/53 and by 1954 they had funds were enough to buy a house, but Sardar Bhil Singh Landa donated 15 Monton Street Moss Side, which he owned to the Gurdwara Sahib. And converted the house into a Gurdwara Sahib with Nishan Sahib in the front garden of the building.

The official inauguration took place on 5th February 1954 with a group photograph of all members Sangat present with one Dr. Jit Singh, a Physician in Manchester Royal Infirmary Hospital, who became the first general secretary of the Gurdwara Sahib. Later, he migrated to Canada. Marble slate at the base of the Nishan Sahib, bears the name of the four respected gentlemen as a mark of respect for the dedicated service to the Sikh community of Manchester which will live forever. First independent Gurdwara established outside of London in the North West of England. The list of all the people who had donated towards this great cause is presented here, although some parts of the original have been lost.

As this was a new venture in Manchester, the city council was proud to have such close-knit community spirit which spread spirituality through humanity. Although churches and synagogues were already present, but Sikh Temples and Mosques were very few. Once it was

Mayor Sir Richard Harper & Lady Mayore's Visiting Gurdwara Sahib 1954

established, it became an icon of the North West. Many dignitaries from England and India visited the Gurdwara Sahib during their tenure of office.

Minister of Punjab Master Tara Singh, Vijay Lakshmai, Lord Mayor and Mayors of Manchester, and many city councillors visited the Gurdwara Sahib from time to time. The Gurdwara Sahib had become a landmark in the North West, making the Bhatra Sikh community a very proud community in every way possible. It now catered for all the Sikh Sangat's religious and cultural needs, celebrating festivals and being able to baptise and marry their children according to Sikh religious rites. The Gurdwara became a focal point for people from surrounding towns in the North West, as they did not have such facilities so near. The establishment of the Gurdwara also became a community centre for people to meet and greet their friends and family, and at the same time take advantage of the religious services which it now provided.

By the 1960s, the Sikh Sangat, especially the Bhatra Sangat, had increased in numbers. Although they lived in groups and in different areas of the city, it was not long before the membership of the Gurdwara also increased. This increment brought about differences of opinions and thought, which culminated into a great split in membership in 1961 when the first group from Hulme became separated from the main Sikh Temple, through disagreement between members. With one group going their separate way, the second group, which lived the farthest from Moss Side, did the same and they also established a Sikh Temple in a house on Halliwell Lane, Cheetham Hill.

It was only a few years down the line when demolition orders came for Hulme and Moss Side. Both areas came under compulsory purchase orders from the city council in 1970 for redevelopment. This meant that Gurdwaras in both areas had to find new places of worship. Guru

The purpose built Gurdwara Sahib Moss side Manchester foundation stone laid by Mayor Fredrick Balcombe JP December 1974

Nanak Nirankari Gurdwara were given a small rundown church building in Piggott Street, off Yarbrough Street Moss Side for a short while, until that also came under the same category of demolition. Again, they were moved to another derelict church building in Gorton area near Bell Vue, which was some distance away from Moss Side and could only be reached by bus or car.

This area was notorious for National Front and other fascist organisations. Having a religious place in this area belonging to an ethnic minority was not safe. It was not long before problems began to occur. The building got broken into on a regular basis, and at one time the culprits set fire to the main prayer hall in which the Holy Guru Granth Sahib Ji was destroyed in the fire.

During this turmoil time at Gorton, the management committee was in consultation with the city council for a plot of land in Moss Side for the construction of a purpose-built Gurdwara. As this Gurdwara was an historic place of worship for the Sikhs, the city council approved a plot of land in Monton Street adjacent to the Christian church. As the houses in the street had now been demolished, this became a through-fare to Lloyd Street, where once was a petrol station. Once the land was approved, the foundation stone was laid by the Lord Mayor of Manchester, Frederick Balcombe JP, in December 1974 and the construction of the purpose-built Gurdwara began. At the same time, the management committee began to collect funds from the Sikh Sangat and businesses as the Gurdwara committee's financial status was limited.

The Sikh Sangat and the businesses donated, but funds were not enough to complete the project. Therefore, the committee decided to approach the city council once again for a community project grant which were being given through the Manpower Services Commission at the time. The main aim of this grant was to reduce the unemployment of manpower through employing labour on these projects. With a condition that no cash from the grant should be used for material cost. Nevertheless, the committee was able to secure a grant of two and a half million pounds to pay the labour force working on the project only.

Obviously, such a big project, the cost would be enormous and the finances were not sufficient. But, on the other hand, most of the main expenses were saved through qualified people who volunteered their services free of charge, like Sardar Amar Singh Egan, Architect, Kuldip Singh Sira, heating engineer, electricians, structural engineers and many others. They all came to offer their help and support in the construction of this historical building.

But still, material costs were high and cash was only minimal. The committee decided to approach the Manpower Services Commission for permission to use the grant money for materials. They agreed on the basis that they had so many volunteers doing the bulk of the work free of charge. As the building was now progressing with a lot of help from the Sikh professionals in the building trade, architect, electricians, structural engineers, heating engineers, plumbing engineers, and many others who offered help in the construction of the building.

In 1972, the Ugandan government under the dictator Idi Amin ordered all Asians to leave the country within 90 days. This ruling had caused a lot of unrest in the East African countries. After World War II, the number of South Asians in East and South Africa increased significantly. These were primarily migrants from Punjab and Gujarat in India. Many of them occupied senior positions in the colonial system in Africa. Not only that, a significant share of the commercial trade in Kenya and Uganda was in the hands of the South Asian settlers.

After the independence of these countries in the 1960s, each country adopted different policies towards the Asian residents. Following Kenya's independence from Britain in 1963, Asians were given two years to acquire Kenyan citizenship to replace the British passports that most

Asians held. However, the majority of them did not take up Kenyan citizenship. The same pattern was repeated in other countries of East and Central Africa. These policies were intended to ensure that the African majority population acquired greater control over key areas of the economy and the government. Many different legislations were passed, including the nationalization of financial institutions, which affected the livelihoods of the Asian community who owned the vast majority of such businesses.

Most of them were Jatts from East Africa and they all put forward a request to become members of the Gurdwara Sahib. This request was put to the management committee, but the committee refused their request. This was a big disappointment to them.

According to Sikh religion, everyone is equal. Guru Gobind Singh Ji, the Tenth Master of the Sikh religion, states, "Manas-Ki-Jaat, Sabhey-Ek-Hi-Paehchanbo" (meaning; all humankind are equal, there should be no difference between people).

However, the deeds of the original Gurdwara had a clause that states, people belonging to the Bhatra sect shall be the sole members of the Gurdwara Sahib. Therefore, the religious belief or the command of the Tenth Master has not prevailed. As we see throughout the world today, there exist many Gurdwaras across the world belonging to different sects of the Sikhs, i.e. Ramgarhia, Ravidas, Ramgharia's, Bhatra, each community group catering for their section of the Sikh community. But they all have one thing in common, that they all adhere to the same scriptures of the Guru Granth Sahib, which has not and will not ever change.

Sikh Association

The origin of the Sikh Association started at the Indian Association Gandhi Hall, a Hindu cultural center based in Withington village in Manchester. The center was named after Mohandas Karamchand Gandhi, an Indian lawyer who led the successful campaign for India's independence from British rule and later inspired movements for civil rights and freedom across the world. The center was founded by Dr. Chatterjee and his colleagues as a Hindu temple (Mandir) to serve the Hindu community. It also celebrated Diwali, Durga Puja, and many other events relating to people of Indian origin. Many members of the Association were also Sikhs. Sardar Amar Singh Egan, a city architect, along with his colleagues, decided to start the Sikh Association within the center and held their own minor events for Sikhs, such as annual dinners and other minor events for his Sikh colleagues.

Parallel to this, the Monton Street Gurdwara was being built with many Sikh professionals who were volunteering their services. Initially, while the construction was ongoing, there were not many member supporters, and they did not participate in any form. They stood aside and waited for the project to collapse and fall flat because they could not digest the success of how the youngsters who were in the forefront managing the project being completed. Instead of being part of the project and participating in the community's success, they started to weave a web of deceit in accusations on the management, which brought about conflict within the community. But a few of the Sewadars were determined in their effort to make a success for the Sikh community.

When the Gurdwara neared completion, this deceitful group made its move and tried to oust the existing organizers and take over the management. Meanwhile, there was certainly a longing among the volunteers that the quarrels would cease, and the real teachings of the gurus would prevail, but this was a never-ending story. Although everyone was hoping and wishing that this Gurdwara would be a monument in the North West of the shire and an icon of the Sikhs, the members had other ideas in their minds. Seeing these quarrels never-ending, the volunteers who were offering their services thought otherwise and sought out an alternative source for their benefit. They started to hold religious ceremonies away from the Gurdwara premises with the view to learn the true message of Guru Ji and away from the quarrels. These gatherings started to take place in Gandhi Hall and later in a hall above Mr. Jaswinder Singh Kohli's business premises on Sherborne Street Manchester. The reason to use this hall was that Mr. Kohli offered it free of cost, whereas the expenses to rent Gandhi Hall were getting difficult, plus there was disturbance from the Hindu worship taking place in the Temple.

This practice continued for some time with tremendous contribution from Gian Inderjit Singh Ji of Derby and Sardar Gurdial Singh Rasia of Birmingham. Then, Mr. Kohli bought the building opposite where the present Gurdwara Siri Harkishan Sahib Ji is, and the Gurdwara was moved into this old clothes mill, which required a complete clearout of old machinery, tables, and so on. This Sewa was taken on by about ten families who dedicated their time and effort to do the clean-out. Because the premises were a working mill, it had a large inbuilt kitchen which came in use for the Gurdwara, and the cleared hall offered more space for the devotees. The religious part was mostly taken care of by Giani Inderjit Singh Ji of Derby, and the congregation started to grow, and the mail started going out under the name of Sikh Association Manchester. The first Amrit Sanchaar in Manchester was held here.

The Gurdwara was operating smoothly until some criticism of the organizers arose claiming that the premises were being treated as the personal property of the owner, and that it should not be subjected to such treatment. As is often the case in Sikh communities, disagreements escalated and the new party sought to remove the existing organizers. They claimed ownership of the contents of the Sikh Association, including the utensils belonging to the Sikh Sangat. This caused tension with the property owner, and the group eventually split and found new premises on Derby Street in Cheetham Hill, which they called the Central Gurdwara. After the split, the owner of the old Sikh Association renamed the Gurdwara as Siri Harkishan Sahib Ji.

This entire scenario started from the Moss Side Gurdwara in the early 1960s when the first split occurred, resulting in not just two but three Gurdwaras in town. The partition movement continued as the Moss Side new purpose-built Gurdwara was nearing completion. Members who had previously ignored its construction started to gather a group together to overthrow those who had put their hearts and souls into the project for the benefit of the Sikh community of Manchester.

However, the group seeking to take over the management did not pay heed to the teachings of the Guru. Taking over was more important to them than supporting the hardworking people who had devoted themselves tirelessly to benefit the entire Sikh community of Manchester and feel proud of their efforts. Unfortunately, their self-centeredness brought shame to a project that had begun with the Guru's blessing.

Sri Guru Gobind Singh Gurdwara Sangat Bhatra Sikh Temple and Mission Centre Rod

Sri Guru Gobind Singh Gurdwara Sangat Bhatra Sikh Temple and Mission Centre Registered. 35 Rosamund Stereet West, Chorlton-on Medlock Manchester 14

In 1961, an altercation between the members of Sri Guru Gobind Singh Gurdwara Sangat Bhatra Sikh Temple and Mission Centre occurred, resulting in the Hulme area members parting company from the main Gurdwara Sahib to establish a Gurdwara in their own area. To finance the project, the members held weekly prayer meetings in each other's homes and collected funds of £1 per member per week, eventually purchasing a house on Rosamund Street West in Chorlton-on-Medlock. The property required renovation to become suitable for worship, which the members completed themselves. The Gurdwara was registered with the city council as a place of worship, and the holy scriptures of Guru Granth Sahib Ji were donated by the elder daughter of Sardar Lahori Singh Berra. Sardar Mokham Singh Potiwal was instated as the first priest of the Gurdwara, and Sardar Mewa Singh Sathi and Pritam Singh Heera from Irlam were in-house Ragis (Hymn singers) who performed the kirtan Sewa every Sunday. The Gurdwara was later transferred to the Whalley Range site and renamed Sri Guru Gobind Singh Gurdwara Sangat Bhatra Mission Centre Regd.

The members of Hulme Gurdwara Sahib

The members of Hulme Gurdwara Sahib included Sr. Mohkam Singh, Sr. Mela Singh Potiwal, Sr. Mangle Singh Potiwal, Sr. Pritam Singh Potiwal, Sr. Jeet Singh Gola, Sr. Gopal Singh Bhaker, Sr. Cheeba Singh Bhaker, Sr. Chiman Singh Mahi, Sr. Darshan Singh Kasbia, Sr. Chiman Singh Swaley, Sr. Lahori Singh Bera, Sr. Sundar Singh Sagar, Sr. Koonan Singh Potiwal, Sr. Dayal Singh Bhaker, Sr. Joginder Singh Potiwal, Sr. Kalyan Singh Digwa, Sr. Bachan Singh Johnny Walker, Sr. Mangal Singh Kasbia, Sr. Mohinder Singh Potiwal, Sr. Kartar Singh Bhaker, Sr. Ranjit Singh Bhaker, Sr. Hardev Singh Digwa, Sr. Kishan Singh Digwa, Sr. Harbans Singh Digwa, Sr. Kuldip Singh Potiwal, Sr. Kuldip Singh Digwa, Sr. Joginder Singh Tiger, Sr. Mohinder Singh Potiwal, Sr. Babu Singh Kasbia, and Sr. Jit Singh Gola. After only eleven years, in 1972, the Hulme area was purchased by the city council under the compulsory purchase order for redevelopment, and the Gurdwara Sahib had to be relocated to Upper Brook Street above the shops. From 1972, the next two to three years were spent in this make-shift building, but most of

Sri Guru Gobind Singh Gurdwara Education & Cultural Centre
Courtesy of Guru Gobind Singh Gurdwara

the members also relocated to the Old Trafford area of the city, which meant they had to travel some distance to the Sikh Temple every Sunday for prayers. It became difficult to have someone attend to Guru Granth Sahib each day. To overcome this problem, the management decided to move nearer home and purchased a property on Upper Chorlton Road, which required major repairs. No sooner had they bought the rundown property than a housing association approached them with a substantial offer to buy it. The members were able to purchase a house across the road, no. 61, and made it suitable for a Gurdwara Sahib. This was now the second Gurdwara established in Manchester belonging to the Bhatra Sangat.

A few years after the community had grown in numbers, a shortage of space became apparent and the management committee decided to build an extension to the building at a cost of £2000. However, even with the extension, the building became too small to accommodate the increasing numbers. In November 2002, an opportunity arose to purchase a larger building, a former car-parts warehouse, at the cost of £320,000, with the intention of building a purpose-built Gurdwara that would cater for future generations.

After five years of exploration, the project was put on hold for a short while due to the recession in 2008/9. However, on August 15th, 2010, India's Independence Day, the foundation stone of the new building was laid by The Panj-Pyares, and a large gathering of Sikhs from all over the UK came to join in the ceremony. The Sikh Sangat raised funds unreservedly, with donations and loans totaling £1.1 million, and a loan of £81,000 was secured from Lloyds Bank.

The Sri Guru Gobind Singh Gurdwara Education & Cultural Centre, located at 57 Upper Chorlton Road, Whalley Range, Manchester M16 7RQ, was opened on November 11th, 2011, with another large gathering of Sikh Sangat attending the ceremony. A short procession (Nagar-Kirtan) took place during the ceremony, and a two-minute silence was observed to remember the war heroes of both World Wars. The officiating Granthis at the opening ceremony were Jatha from Patiala, India, including Bhai Harvinder Singh, Bhai Sukhwinder Singh, and Bhai Jagdeep Singh.

The opening day was marked by honouring the people who had given their services to the project, including building contractors, structural engineers, electricians, architects, and all those who played a vital part in making this exceptional project a reality. The new purpose-built Gurdwara Sahib was renamed in honor of its opening.

The opening ceremony of the new purpose built Gurdwara held on 11th November 2011 again with a large gathering of Sikh Sangat from all over the UK came to attend the ceremony. For the ceremony, a short procession (Nagar-Kirtan) took place and during the procession a two minute silence was observed in respect of remembering our war heroes of both World-Wars. The officiating Granthis at that time of opening ceremony was Jatha from Patiala India, Bhai Harvinder Singh, and Bhai Sukhwinder Singh Bhai Jagdeep Singh. The opening day was marked with honouring people who gave their abnegating services to the project. Building contractors, structural engineers, electricians, architects, and all the people who played a vital part in making this exceptional project into a reality The new purpose built Gurdwara Sahib was renamed.

Bhai Harvinder Singh, Bhai Sukhwinder Singh & Bhai Sukhsagar Singh

Dashmesh Sikh Temple Cheetham hill Manchester UK

Gurdwara Deshmesh Sikh Temple Cheetham Hill. Courtesy of Dashemesh Gurdwara

The Dashmesh Sikh Temple in Cheetham Hill, Manchester, UK, was established by a small group of Sikhs who lived far from Moss Side. After splitting from the main establishment, the Cheetham Hill group saw this as a golden opportunity to establish their own Gurdwara Sahib. Despite being a small group with no funds, Sardar Khazan Singh Landa provided one of his houses at 107 Halliwell Lane as the base for the Gurdwara Sahib. The group members worked to make the house suitable for worship, and thus the origins of the third Gurdwara in the city were established.

The elder members took on the Sunday service duties themselves, but after a year or so, the area came under a council compulsory purchase order for redevelopment, leaving the Cheetham Hill Sangat in a dilemma. They had to quickly find a building to relocate to, without any help from the city council. They hired local church halls for their Sunday worship and even held marriage ceremonies there. Eventually, they purchased a building on Heywood Street, renovated it to make it suitable for Gurdwara Sahib, and registered it as a place of worship and marriage ceremonies. They named it Gurdwara Dashmesh Darbar Sikh Temple.

Group members:- Sr. Khazan Singh Landa, Sr. Kuldip Singh Landa, Sr. Iqbal Singh Landa, Sr. Shingar Singh Sangi, Sr. Avtar Singh Sangi, Sr. Dildar Singh Sangi, Sr. Jit Singh Bhaker, Sr. Baldev Singh Bhaker, Sr. Sukhdev Singh Bhaker, Sr. Gurbachan Singh Roudh, Sr. Avtar Singh Roudh, Sr. Walati Singh Roudh, Sr. Charanjit Singh Potiwal, Sr. Jaswant Singh Kasbia, Sher Singh Bhaker, Sr. Singh Bhaker, Sr. Harbhajan Singh Bhaker, Sr., Sr. Kushwant Singh, Sr. Dalwant Singh Rador, Sr. Gurbax Singh Rador, Sr. Balwant Singh, Sr. Niranjan Singh Bhaker, Sr. Waryam Singh Bhaker. Sr. Chanan Singh.

Within a span of only about four years, three Sikh Temples were established in Manchester, all operating within the code and conduct of the Sikh religion and managed by the Bhatra Sikhs. It's noteworthy that since their arrival in England in the early 1920s, they have always kept their identity intact by not cutting their long hair or shaving their long beards, and adhering to religious principles. Although they were now separated into three different groups, having Gurdwaras nearer home to cater for their group, they still intermingled in other functions and celebrations as one big family, never forgetting that they were an interrelated community. Whenever it became necessary to support each other in any community affairs, they never hesitated to do so. A proof of their solidarity spirit became apparent when they supported the Turban case with Manchester Corporation Transport Department, which refused to employ Sikhs on the buses. All the three Gurdwaras came together in support of the struggle for employment by presenting petitions, attending meetings with the transport committee, and lobbying at council offices. There is photo evidence available in archives. Furthermore, this solidarity of oneness became historic when the three Gurdwaras formed a Gurdwara committee named Sangat Bhatra Committee of Manchester to celebrate important religious functions.

Sangat Bhatra Committee of Manchester

In 1967, all three Gurdwaras organized a meeting and decided to form an alliance committee named the Sangat Bhatra Committee of Manchester. The committee's aim was to organize the upcoming Gurpurabs of the Sikh Gurus, with a focus on the fast-approaching important 300th birthday Gurpurab of the tenth Master, Guru Gobind Singh Ji. The committee consisted of several members, including Sr. Mangal Singh Potiwal, Sr. Kalyan Singh Digwa, Sr. Fauja Singh Rangela, Sr. Mehar Singh Rador, Sr. Gopal Singh Bhaker, Sr. Harbhajan Singh Bhaker, Sr. Mehar Singh Pardesi (priest), Sr. Mewa Singh Sathi, Sr. Shingar Singh Sangi, Sr. Gurbax Singh Aziz, Sr. Pritam Sing Rasila, Sr. Mela Singh Potiwal, Sr. Rattan Pal Singh Landa, Sr. Tirath Singh Rador, Sr. Dayal Singh Bhaker, Sr. Lahori Sing Kalnoria, Sr. Dalip Singh Digwa, Sr. Kuldip Singh Deepak, Sr. Lahori Singh Berra, Sr. Koonan Singh Potiwal, Sr. Ranjit Singh, Sr. Charnjeet Singh Bhaker, Sr. Chiman Singh Mahi, Sr. Kuldip Singh wonderful, Sr. Sewa Singh Himat, Gyani Sundar Singh Sagar, and Sr. Mohkam Singh Potiwal.

On May 21, 1967, the committee set about organizing the 300th birthday celebrations of Guru Gobind Singh Ji, and due to the joint effort of the three Gurdwaras, the celebration took place at All Saints Town Hall, located near the Rosamund Street Gurdwara Sahib. Prominent people from outer towns also took part in the celebrations, such as Sr. Zhanda Singh Patel and Sr. Harnam Singh Koumi from Cardiff, Gian Makhan Singh Mirgind from London, Gyani Sundar Singh Sagar from Manchester, Sr. Jang Ji from Bristol, Gyani Tripat Ji from Cardiff, Sr. Mangal Singh Majhel from Preston, Sr. Santokh Singh Bristol, and Gyani Ratan Singh Shaad from Bristol.

The visitors from other towns saw the success of the event and gathered themselves together to request the organizing committee to arrange a meeting of all Bhat Sikhs in the UK to form a one platform from which issues arising in the community can be addressed. However, the committee did not take any action on this matter, and nearly two years passed with no progress made by any organization or individual city.

In 1969, the 500th birthday of the founder Guru of the Sikh religion, Guru Nanak Dev Ji, arrived, and the committee came together again to organize the celebration. The committee decided to celebrate this once-in-a-lifetime event on a large scale so that Sangat from sur-rounding towns and cities could participate. The venue for this historic celebration was Manchester Free Trade Hall Peter Street Manchester, and the event took place in May 1970 with great flamboyance. People from all walks of life were invited to give speeches on the life of Guru Nanak Dev Ji.

After seeing the success for the second time, many visitors from outer towns, especially from the Bhat community, arranged a meeting at Guru Nanak Dev Ji Gurdwara in Moss Side. The consensus of the meeting was to approach the Sangat Bhatra committee of Manchester and request them to call for an all-UK Bhatra conference. With this in mind, they organized a meeting with the Sangat Bhatra committee of Manchester and put forward their request.

The Conference

After some deliberation, the organising committee accepted the re-quest and began organizing a two-day conference in Manchester, set for October 18th and 19th, 1970. The conference was to be held at St. Gerard's Hall, Denmark Road, Moss Side, near Guru Nanak Nirankari Gurdwara Monton Street, which was designated as the HQ. Organiz-ing such a large event required hard work and dedicated people, and although the Manchester Sangat had experience organizing big events, this one was new and unpredictable in terms of the number of attend-ees. Therefore, the committee faced the challenge of finding a large venue, arranging accommodation for guests, financing the event, and providing food.

To address these challenges, the organizing committee decided to use Guru Nanak Nirankari Gurdwara and Guru Gobind Singh Gurd-wara Rosamund Street West for accommodation, depending on the number of attendees. Two gentlemen, Sardar Mangal Singh Potiwal of Manchester and Sardar Harnam Singh Koumi of Cardiff, volunteered to finance the entire project, but the organizing committee felt that it should be financed by Guru Nanak Nirankari Gurdwara with donations from Sangat as it was a national event. Nevertheless, the two gentlemen were thanked for their offer.

For the duration of the conference, sewadars from prominent Jathe-dar's, Sardar Tirath Singh Rador, Sardar Gopal Singh Bhaker, and Sar-dar Mehar Singh Rador, took on the service of preparing food for the

Sangat, offering their abnegating service to the community. These three gentlemen never left the kitchen and provided Langar day and night.

During the conference, many issues were discussed, and ways to tackle them were explored. One of the main issues was the need for a governing body and headquarters of the society. As Manchester was spearheading the conference, it was discussed that Manchester should be at the forefront, but a decision could not be reached due to differing opinions. Near the end of the second day, it was decided by majority that a governing body of Bhatra board should be formed. The formation of the board and its office bearers would be elected in the next conference, and Birmingham Sangat volunteered to hold it at their Gurdwara Sahib.

Many discussions took place between participating towns and individual members before the Birmingham conference, but unfortunately, not many people attended the conference due to disagreements. Thus, all the efforts of the Sangat Bhatra committee of Manchester went to waste, despite their valuable time and effort.

Sardar Bhil Singh Landa

Sardar Bhil Singh Landa

This is a historical account of the Sikh community in Manchester and the contributions made by Sardar Bhil Singh Landa, a pioneer businessman and property owner. The story begins in Moss Side Manchester, an area with a multicultural community of people of different denominations, including Sikhs, Muslims, West Indians, and Jewish people. Despite their differences, they lived together in harmony as one family.

Sardar Bhil Singh Landa was born on April 13th, 1895, in Lahore, now in Pakistan. He received his education at a local village school and married Bibi Sant Kour of Bhaker clan at the age of 20. They had eight children. With the support of his family, Sardar Bhil Singh started various business ventures, including a flour mill and a timber merchant. He also worked as a bus driver before leaving his business to his children and traveling to South Africa with his elder brother, Lahori Singh, as a cloth merchant for 16 years.

He visited the UK in 1937, residing in London, Glasgow, and Edinburgh. However, he had to return to India in 1938 due to his wife's passing, leaving young children behind. In 1940, he remarried Lajwanti Kour in Gujranwala, Pakistan. The partition of India in 1947 gave him and his family the opportunity to migrate to England as refugees, settling in New York Street in the Hulme area of Manchester.

Sardar Bhil Singh and his family brought with them a small "Gutka" or a Sri Guru Granth Sahib Ji, a small volume of Sikh prayers, when they migrated to England on a ship. As a devoted Sikh, this was dear to his family. They later moved to Moss Side, where they bought a house in Monton Street and installed the Guru Granth Sahib Ji in their home, holding weekly prayers on Sundays. They invited other Sikh families to join them in their prayers, which became a regular weekly event.

Sardar Bhil Singh continued to expand his business portfolio, including a manufacturing business, property investments, and opening the first Asian groceries shop in Monton Street, Moss Side. He was known for his kind and helping nature, always extending his hand to those in need. He also promoted his faith by opening his doors to all Sangat for prayers.

The Landa family had the privilege of hosting the Lord Mayor and Mayoress of Manchester, Mr. Leslie Lever and his wife, at their residence during this period. They also welcomed many other dignitaries, including Vijay Laxmi, the high commissioner of India to Britain and Ireland in 1955, who was received by Sardar Bhil Singh Landa and other Manchester Sikhs.

Overall, the story highlights the contributions made by Sardar Bhil Singh Landa and the Sikh community in Manchester and their dedication to their faith and community.

Inauguration of Gurdwara

During a Sunday congregation at their residence, the Sangat decided to establish a Gurdwara in Manchester. To achieve this goal, they formed a thirteen-member committee. The members of the committee were as follows:

1. Sardar Khazan Singh Bhaker – President of Sewak Jatha Manchester

2. Sardar Sant Singh Pardesi - Vice President of Khalsa Jatha London

3. Sardar Bhil Singh Landa - General Secretary of Sewak Jatha Manchester

4. Sardar Dolat Singh Potiwal - Vice President of Sewak Jatha Manchester

5. Sardar Jagjit Singh Prof - University of Manchester
6. Sardar Chiba Singh Bhaker - Manchester
7. Sardar Ajit Singh Bhatu - Cashier of Sewak Jatha Manchester
8. Sardar Lahori Singh Rador
9. Sardar Pheru Singh Landa
10. Sardar Balwant Singh Digwa
11. Sardar Mohkam Singh Potiwal
12. Sardar Ram Singh Gouzra
13. Sardar Mela Singh Potiwal

Four members of the committee were selected to collect funds for the Gurdwara Sahib. They began touring England on November 20th, 1953, and visited nearly all the towns. The collection continued until 1954. At the time, most of the Sikh people residing in the UK were of the Bhatra tribe, and they contributed unconditionally. Their contributions were greatly appreciated, and their names and amounts were registered. The list was proudly displayed in the main prayer hall of the Gurdwara Sahib.

On April 13th, 1954, the day of the birth of Khalsa (Vaisakhi), the Gurdwara Sahib was inaugurated with the Sewa of Nishan Sahib in the forecourt of the Gurdwara Sahib. The above-named thirteen-member committee was elected to the management committee, and it was named the Sewak Jatha of Manchester. Three people were chosen to make the rules and regulations for the Gurdwara Sahib. They were Sardar Chiba Singh Bhaker, Sardar Bhil Singh Landa, and Sardar Bhadur Singh Bhaker. These regulations are now in the records of the Gurdwara Sahib.

In August 1954, Master Tara Singh, the President of Shiromani Gurdwara Parbandhak Committee (SGPC) Amritsar India, visited England. The Manchester Sikh Sangat invited him to visit the Gurdwara Sahib, which was the second Gurdwara Sahib in the United Kingdom. He was warmly welcomed, and the President Khazan Singh Bhaker presented him with £101 pounds. Gyani Sundar Singh Sagar read a memorandum demanding rights for the Bhatra ethnic group in India. The main aim of the donation was to promote Sikh literature in Europe. Many living in England at the time believed that Sikhs were becoming clean-shaven (Patit) due to not finding employment while wearing their turbans. Therefore, it was necessary to raise awareness of Sikh religion and its ethics.

However, Sardar Bhil Singh Ji had already written a letter to Master Tara Singh, the leader of SGPC Amritsar, about his promise of promoting Sikh religion, but nothing had been done. Sardar Bhil Singh took it upon himself to visit India and Pakistan.

Bhil Singh Landa visits India & Pakistan

In September 1958, Sardar Bhil Singh embarked on a journey to visit India and Pakistan via ship. He arrived in Bombay on September 24th of that year and began his trip by visiting Sikh shrines. Later, he arranged meetings with Master Tara Singh, his secretary, and other individuals to discuss the promotion of Sikhism. Despite several attempts, it wasn't until November 2nd of that year that Sardar Bhil Singh was finally able to meet with Master Tara Singh. During their discussion, they talked about Sikh missionary work in Europe. The meeting concluded with Sardar Bhil Singh writing to the chief editors of Akali and Parbhat newspapers for assistance with his cause. Afterward, Sardar Bhil Singh traveled to Pakistan to visit his place of birth and reconnect with friends. During his visits to the Gurudwaras in the village, he discovered that the buildings had been locked for so long that they were in a state of disrepair. The same was true of the Gurudwara Dera Sahib, where the fifth Guru Arjan Dev Ji was martyred. Throughout his visit to both countries, Sardar Bhil Singh discussed issues with various dignitaries in hopes of achieving results. Unfortunately, his efforts came to no avail.

In the last week of February 1959, Sardar Bhil Singh met with Sardar Karam Singh Jakhmi, the chief editor of Akali, in Jalandhar city. During the meeting, he provided photos of the Lord Mayor of Manchester's visit to the Manchester Gurudwara Sahib and discussed issues regarding the difficulties faced by Sikhs and the promotion of Sikhism. The photos were published in the paper.

While in India, Sardar Bhil Singh visited other towns and cities where the Bhatra Sangat lived. He realized that they had not been able to demand their rights fully and required a platform to make their case and demand their citizen's rights, as they had been labeled as a backward caste.

As a result of his visits and discussions, a request was made by the Patiala Bhatra Sangat to hold a conference of all India Bhat Bradri. The town of Ragu Majra, near Patiala city, was chosen for the conference, and the date was set for February 6th, 1959.

The All India Bhatra Bradri Conference was attended by many prominent people from towns all over India. The conference passed resolutions regarding their citizenship status in the Indian constitution. The Bhatra tribe was classified as a backward class, and there was a unanimous vote to present a petition to the then Punjab chief minister, Sardar Pratap Singh Karo, in Chandigarh.

On February 11th, 1959, a deputation that included Sardar Bhil Singh Landa went to Chandigarh and presented the petition to the chief minister. The chief minister promised them that their demands would be met, and backward classes would receive priority in gaining employment and education.

All of this was achieved with the efforts of Sardar Bhil Singh Landa, who had gone from England with the aim of gaining support from Sikh leaders. Though he had not been successful in securing Master Tara Singh's support, Sardar Bhil Singh's perseverance, along with the help of the Bhatra Sangat India, ultimately resulted in the classification of their citizenship and the rights that came with it.

Return to England

During his ten long month tour of India and Pakistan he struggled to get support from any of the Sikh leaders. Disappointed he returned to England but, before returning he purchased a full set of printing presses which he brought back to UK. Once back in Manchester he started a monthly magazine called "Sikh Missionary Manchester" with the support of Sardar Shingar Singh Sangi as his assistant editor The first and only publication of the magazine was published in November 1959 on the birth anniversary of Guru Nanak Dev Ji. His next aim was to publish next publication in English but it was not to be. On page twenty five of the magazine, he documents the full story of his tour and all the meetings held with leaders. With determination and effort anyone can achieve anything for themselves but, Sardar Bhil Singh's fortitude was for his religion and his faith. A person of great stature propagating community spirit, preaching spirituality, spreading faith to wider community, co-founder of first Gurdwara outside London, a business man, manufacturer, importer and exporter, property landlord and above all person of integrity and empathy who gave his all to the Sikh community of Manchester and breathed his last breath in the presence of Guru

Granth Sahib in November 1964 while lecturing on the life of Guru Nanak Dev Ji's birthday within the Gurdwara which he was co-founder of.

Gyani Mehar Singh Pardesi first Sikh high Priest Manchester Gurdwara

Gyani Mehar Singh Pardesi First Sikh high Priest Guru Nanak
Nirankari Gurdwara Moss Side, Manchester 1954-1970

Gyani Mehar Singh Pardesi was the first Sikh high priest of Manchester Gurdwara. He arrived in England on a ship named S.S. Multan, which docked at Tilbury docks in London in August 1948 from Bombay (now Mumbai). Born in Glotian, Kalan, a village in the district of Dashka (now in Pakistan) on 3rd November 1917, he received his education in the village school where he learned the Urdu language. Soon after, he joined the local Gurdwara classes from where he learned his mother tongue Punjabi language from the head priest Bhai Isher Singh Swaley.

Later, when his elder brother Hansa Singh died at their ancestral home in the state of Jammu Kashmir district Udhampur, he moved to his parental home in the village of Garhi. This was not densely populated at the time. Nevertheless, his father Pandit Nanak Singh, a village elder, was well known throughout the local district of Udhampur for his knowledge of Hindu rituals and was well-educated in palmistry and Ayurvedic medicine. Respected by Hindu Brahmins (Pandits), Nanak Singh was held in very high esteem, and revered as their leader.

Although Mehar Singh was well-versed with the Hindu religion and its rituals, he was also an ardent believer in the Sikh religion. In their house, they had Guru Granth Sahib Ji installed in a special room and used it as their prayer room. After a few years living with his parents, Mehar Singh accompanied his elder brother Lall Singh to Darjeeling Kalipong, where they took residence in a Hindu Mandir, and he became a disciple of Pandit Dogra Mal. From him, Mehar Singh learned Hindi language while doing Sewa in the Mandir, at the same time enlightened them about Sikh ideals. Being a virtuous person, he became well known in the locality of Kalipong. While in Kalipong, he also became friends with a Gorkha motor garage owner and requested him to train his nephew who was interested in motor mechanics.

Once the garage owner agreed, his nephew Joginder Singh was called over from Patiala to Darjeeling and began his training as a motor mechanic. After a few years of training, when he was capable and fully trained as a mechanic, he came back to Patiala and set up his own motor mechanic workshop on Mall Road Patiala. After his arrival in England in 1948 until 1952, Mehar Singh worked as a door-to-door salesman, moving around different towns and cities looking for better business. In 1952, he came to Manchester and found work in a manufacturing company based in the Collyhurst area of Manchester.

During the next two years, Sardar Bhil Singh Landa, also a resident of Manchester and a devoted Sikh, held prayers in their home each Sunday, where Mehar Singh presided over the services. After two years, the movement for the establishment of a Gurdwara in the town started, and by 1954, the first Gurdwara in Manchester had been established. The inauguration had taken place, and as with all Sikh Gurdwaras, a priest in attendance of the Guru Granth Sahib was always necessary. There being no one experienced enough to take on the duties, the four elders who were the core founders of the Sikh Temple and now the management committee of the Gurdwara Sahib - Sardar Bhil Singh Landa, Sardar Khazan Singh Bhaker, Sardar Sant Singh Pardesi, and Sardar Mela Singh Bhaker - approached Mehar Singh Pardesi to become their priest of the Gurdwara Sahib in 1954 when he was officially stated the first Sikh priest of Guru Nanak Nirankari Gurdwara, managed by the Sewak Jatha of Manchester, located at 15 Monton Street, Moss Side, Manchester 15. Telephone number MOS 4593.

Now that the Gurdwara had been established, the community was proud to have the facilities at their doorstep to worship and celebrate festivals which they could not before. With this, the community gained the freedom to ascertain other cultural needs such as baptizing their newborn children and performing the ceremony of marrying their siblings in their town.

The needs of the community were very minimal at the time, and the same principle was applied that services were held each Sunday, being the main prayer day of the week. The Sangat used to gather from Cheetham Hill and Hulme, as they all were now members of the Gurdwara Sahib. Because of only Sunday services, the priest carried on working in a factory as well as his priestly duties as required by the management. During his services to the Sikh community, he also took on the roles of many other posts in the management committee. A few years later, the management committee, recognizing the services of their priest, bestowed the honor of "Gyani Ji" - status of high priest.

Being the only Gurdwara in the North West, people from all walks of life came to the congregation each Sunday, regardless of their faith and beliefs. My personal experience of the 60s is that a Muslim wrestler who was from Panja Sahib, the birthplace of Guru Nanak Dev Ji, used to attend the congregation every Sunday morning.

He was so dedicated that every Sunday he would arrive early in the morning and stay until the end of the day's services. Despite being a free-style wrestler by profession and a diabetic, he would accept the Parshad (a sweet sanctified-pudding) distributed to the congregation at the end of the services as a blessing and eat the whole portion, even though his Sikh friends and the priest advised him not to, saying that it could harm his health. But he would reply, "If I am to die, what better way than with Guru's blessing?"

As a Sikh priest, Gyani Ji took part in many Sikh issues which arose from time to time, one of the most prominent being the Sikh Turban case with the Manchester City Transport Department. They were reluctant to employ Turban-wearing Sikhs as bus drivers and conductors. Once the case was won, his elder son Mukhtiar Singh Pardesi became the first Sikh bus conductor on the Manchester Corporation Transport Department on February 7, 1967.

During his long service as Granthi of the Gurdwara Sahib, he was always at the forefront of bringing the community together. There are many times and occasions to be remembered during the 60s and 70s when, in the cold weather, the Sangat would gather with determination to celebrate and commemorate each occasion together. Every Sunday's congregation, which was attended by Sangat from the Cheetham Hill and Hulme areas, would gather and congregate with friends and relatives at the end of the service, and the sacred Karah-Parshad (consecrated sweet pudding) would be distributed abundantly. Everyone always wanted a second helping, but nowadays they prefer smaller portions due to their fear of sugar and diabetes. Then came the hot tea and Pakora's served in brown bags to the entire congregation.

The tea was served in brown ex-American army mugs, and the Pakoras used to go in their duffel coat pockets to be eaten during the Indian film interval. The only cinema showing Indian films on Sunday afternoons was on Denmark Road, near Manchester Royal Infirmary, which later became the Chest Clinic of Manchester Royal Infirmary. In 1969, Granada TV Studios made a documentary for schools called "Our Neighbours." An educational program for school children to learn about other religions and cultures of different people residing in Manchester. The Sikh version of the documentary was filmed in the Gurdwara Sahib during the children being taught their mother tongue Punjabi. The documentaries of all the communities were shown on national TV in their schools' programs.

Just about a year later, in November 1970, Gyani Ji was returning home for his lunch from the Gurdwara Sahib when he was struck with a heart attack. He was admitted to the hospital where he passed away on November 6, 1970.

Gyani Mehar Singh Pardesi was a respected Sikh priest who served the community for sixteen years before his sudden passing. His funeral was attended by many from around the district, and a memorial service was held on March 16, 1971, to honour his long service to Gurdwara Sahib and the community. The service included an Akhand Padh and Kirtan by Harbhajan Singh Mouji, and was followed by a showing of the Our Neighbours documentary filmed at the Gurdwara Sahib.

At St Gerrads Hall, there were two sessions of eulogy and speeches, with invited guests and dignitaries paying tribute to Gyani Mehar Singh Pardesi's dedicated service to the Sikh community of Manchester. In the first session, speakers included Sardar Puran Singh, Gyani Makhan Singh Mirgind, Gyani Sundar Singh Sagar, Mrs Kailash Puri,

Dr Gopal Singh Puri, Muslim High Priest Mr. Noorldin, Mr. Sewa Singh Himat, Mr. Gurbax Singh Aziz, and Mr. Shingar Singh Sangi. In the second session, host dignitaries such as the Dean of Manchester, the Assistant High Commissioner of India, Father Christi from Liverpool, City Councillor Mr. Bolan Manchester, and the manager of the Almond factory where Gyani Ji worked, paid tribute in English.

Gyani Mehar Singh Pardesi's elder son, Mr. Mukhtiar Singh Pardesi, was presented with an inscribed Siri Sahib (sword) and Dastar (turban) tribute by the Guru Nanak Nirankari Gurdwara and its management committee in honour of his father's service to the Sikh community. The President of Akali-Dal UK, Gyani Makhan Singh Mirgind, also presented a Dastar in respect of Gyani Mehar Singh Pardesi's Sewa.

Jathedar Sardar Tirath Singh Rador

The Sikh religion is based on three principles laid down by the founder Guru Nanak Dev Ji: Kirat Karo, Naam Japo, and Wand Chako. Kirat Karo, which means living by one's honest labours, is the basic belief of a Sikh. Sharing one's income or food is also very important. Naam Japo or Simaran promotes love for all creation and concentration on the holy Nam. Wand Chako, which means "earn your living and share it with others," is another important principle.

Sardar Tirath Singh Rador was born in Amritsar, India, on 11th March 1903 to parents Baag Singh Rajjotshi and Mata Kartar Kour. After travelling to many countries with his elder brother Inder Singh Shashtry, they came to the UK in 1937. Unfortunately, at the start of the Second World War in 1938, they had to return to India. Sardar Tirath Singh returned to the UK in 1948 and settled in Cheetham Hill, Manchester. Later his family joined him with their children. His elder son Sewa Singh Himat gained a degree in machine shop engineering, and his younger brother Kuldip Singh became a member of Physics BSc pharmacy.

Sardar Tirath Singh Rador's dedication to his religion is an example to the Manchester Sikh Sangat. He used to say, "Sewa is done not in front of Sangat but behind them." His dedication in the newly established Gurdwara Sahib in 1954 started with the first Akhand-Padh Sahib celebration in honour of the inauguration of the opening ceremony of Gurdwara Sahib in the North West. Sardar Tirath Singh began his journey of Sewa in the Gurdwara kitchen, preparing Langar. He would arrive at the Gurdwara Sahib early in the morning from Cheetham Hill to start the Langar preparation, and from then on, he would never leave the premises until the end of the ceremony. Even during the night, he would make sure that the Padhi's awakened on time for their shift and provide refreshments for them every two hours.

Sardar Tirath Singh Rador's Langar Sewa was highly appreciated by the Sikh community, and he was bestowed with the honour of head Jathedar by the management committee of Guru Nanak Nirankari Gurdwara, managed by the Sewak Jatha of Manchester Monton Street, Moss Side. His colleagues Sardar Gopal Singh Bhaker and Mehar Singh Rador also participated in the Sewa during the festivities, but Sardar Tirath Singh carried out the Sewa for the entire duration, including night shifts. During the 1960s and 1970s, central heating systems were not common, and the only way to heat homes was through coal fire, which also heated water. Despite harsh weather conditions such as heavy snow and smog (fog), Sardar Tirath Singh and his companions were determined to provide Langar to the Sangat every day and night. They showed remarkable commitment and dedication, which even younger individuals would find challenging to match. He travelled by bus from Cheetham Hill every time, regardless of the weather. Sardar Tirath Singh believed that Guru Ji's grace and blessings were with him and inspired him to carry out Sewa for the community's benefit. During the redevelopment of Moss Side and Hulme areas, he played a vital role in collecting funds for the purpose-built Gurdwara Sahib. Unfortunately, during the construction of the new building, Sardar Tirath Singh fell ill and could not see its completion. He passed away on 25th April 1976. A memorial service was held for him, and an Akhand-Padh Sahib was conducted in the community hall of the Gurdwara Sahib, which was still under construction at the time. It was the first Akhand-Padh Sahib held to honour Sardar Tirath Singh Rador's 22 years of service to the Sikh community and the Gurdwara Sahib. On 11th, 12th, and 13th August 1978, the Manchester Sangat paid their respects to Jathedar Tirath Singh Rador for his virtuous Sewa to the community.

Gyani Sundar Singh Sagar and the Manchester Turban Case

Gyani Sundar Singh Sagar religious advisor
Manchester Sikh Temples

Gyani Sundar Singh Sagar was born on June 3rd, 1917, in the village of Ghalotian Kalan, located in the Sialkot district of Punjab, India (now Pakistan). He received his education from Scot Mission High School and graduated from Punjab University Amritsar, where he studied Punjabi language and literature. During his time at university, Gyani Ji married Rajendra Kaur in 1938 and earned a Hons degree in Punjabi language and literature soon after. While still in Sialkot, he actively participated in social work and helped establish the Sarab Hind Bhatra Union, an association that aimed to manage and represent the affairs of the Bhat community and promote it on a wider scale.

The formation of the Sarab Hind Bhatra Union was in its early stages when the partition of India and Pakistan occurred in 1947. The split caused devastation for both countries, and Gyani Ji's family relocated to Amritsar from Ghalotian during the ensuing disorder. They settled in the city and made it their home. Some of Gyani Ji's former friends had already migrated to England and formed an association called the Changa-Bhatra-Nau-Jawan-Sabha UK on August 15th, 1939.

In 1948, Gyani Sundar Singh Sagar immigrated to England with his father, Sardar Haiba Singh Ji, and settled in Manchester, where he worked as a salesman with pioneering spirit. Gyani Ji never lost his valour and continued to fight for the rights of his fellow countrymen. He began campaigning for Turban-wearing Sikhs to be employed as bus drivers and conductors in Manchester, motivated by his religious faith and strong beliefs.

This 9-10 year-long journey started in 1959 when Gyani Ji applied for a job as a bus conductor at MCTD's headquarters, Bus Depot Devonshire Street, Ardwick Manchester. Although he passed the test, he was refused employment on the grounds that he would have to wear a full uniform, including a peaked cap, which would force him to abandon his Turbans. As a Sikh, Gyani Sundar Singh Sagar could not cut his hair and wear a cap or hat, as long uncut hair and beard are symbols of the Sikh faith ordained by the tenth master, Guru Gobind Singh Ji, in 1699. Wearing a Turban was a way to keep his hair clean and tidy.

The refusal to employ him based on his Turban was considered discriminatory against the Sikh religion. Therefore, Gyani Ji began a decade-long battle with the Manchester Corporation Transport Department and City Council to lift the discriminatory ban. During his struggle, he produced a dossier on the merits of Sikhs and their sacrifices made in the First and Second World Wars to gather support for his campaign.

The Dossier of Sikhs and Turban

During the First and Second World Wars, Sikhs served in the British Indian Army under the British Raj. They wore their Turbans into battle and were awarded many gallantry awards. However, years later, when Sikhs living in Britain applied for jobs, they were often refused employment because of their Turbans. One such example was the Manchester Corporation Transport Department, which refused to employ Sikhs as bus drivers or conductors because they had to wear a uniform hat, which was against their religious beliefs.

Gyani Sundar Singh Sagar, an academic in Punjabi literature and religious advisor to Manchester Sikh Temples, applied for employment with the transport department but was refused on the grounds that he could not wear his Turban. This was discrimination against the Sikh faith, and Gyani Ji was determined to fight for the rights of Sikhs to wear their Turbans while working on Manchester council buses.

After years of struggling with the authorities and gathering support, including producing a dossier and pamphlets outlining the basics of the Sikh religion and the Sikh Turban, and the sacrifices of Sikh soldiers in the British Indian Army, Gyani Ji and his supporters finally succeeded in their campaign. They lobbied and rallied support from many councillors, MPs, ex-soldiers who had served in the forces with Sikh regiments, and members of three Sikh Temples. They also gathered a petition, which was presented to the Lord Mayor of Manchester at Manchester Town Hall.

In August 1960, a twelve-page dossier titled "The Sikh and Turban" and a five-page deputation petition were presented at a meeting with the Manchester Corporation Transport Department (MCTD).

Sikhs and Turbans: The Dossier

The Sikh, a small well knit community of fewer than eight million people, is unique in the religious civilization of the world. Practical and progressive in their outlook, they are deeply attached to their faith. Religious belief is their living impulse and the main spring of their national characteristics and history.

The Sikh, are deeply devoted people and faith is an essential trait of their nature. An immense reserve of spiritual energy has been their strong asset in many a crises during their 500 year old history.

They must not, of course smoke, nor cut or trim their hair or beards. These are inviolable injunctions of Sikhs' discipline as lay down by the Guru and are followed by the faithful with reverence due to the master's command.

The essential fact about Sikhs is the moral prestige they have built up by their steadfast and often severely trying adherence to their religious faith.

The heritage of the Sikhs By Harbans Singh

Sikhism is the only religion in the history of the world which has given birth to a nation

World's living religions by Robert E. Hume

The distinctive outward features of the Khalsa religion are the uncut hair and the beard. Wearing the hair and beard has been a tradition among Indian ascetics. By making this obligatory, Guru Gobind Singh intended to emphasis the ideal of ascetic saintliness and to raise an army of soldiers-saints. It is also likely that, by making his followers easily recognizable by virtue of their Turbans and beards. The Guru wanted to raise a body of men who would not be able to deny their faith when *in danger but whose external appearance would invite persecution and, in turn, breed courage to resist it.*

The Sikhs today by Khushwant Singh

The Sikh gurus had all let their hair and beards grow to their natural length, but had not insisted that all of their follower should do the same. They had relied on example alone in the matter — Guru Gobind Singh perceived the paramount necessity of giving his saint soldier a distinct appearance along with their unique personality. Subsequently, he ordained that uncut hair and flowing beard should be on the head and face of every one of his followers. None who disobey him in this vital particular could call him a Sikh.

Life of Guru Gobind Singh by Kartar Singh M.A

To the new holy order the Guru Gobind Singh gave his own personality of beard and hair with Turbans on.

A brief sketch of Guru Gobind Singh by Trilochan Singh

Turbans must be worn and the long hair let down and combed at least twice a day. Granth Sahib or sacred writing, must be read morning and evening, and if possible before meals.

The Sikh of Punjab by R. E. Parry

Guru Gobind Singh introduced the curiously distinctive custom of not cutting the hair or beard and prohibited the use of tobacco — apparently as outward signs by which the Sikhs should be recognized as such. Under no circumstances, not even to save his life in fever, will a Sikh allow his hair to be cut.

Transformation of Sikhism by Sir G. C. Narang

Although Guru Gobind Singh allowed his Sikhs to adopt the dress of every country they inhabit, yet they must not wear hats but "Turbans" to confine the long hair they are strictly enjoined to preserve.

The Sikh Religion by M. A. McAuliffe

"A Sikh is never to wear a cap or hat, not to shave his beard or cut his hair, he is never to take his Turban off whilst taking food.

Translation of Adi-Granth by Dr. Ernest Trump

Locks should remain unshorn. They should all name themselves Singh.

History of the Sikh by J. D. Cunningham

Guru Gobind Singh 1666-1708 tenth and the last human Guru raised all Sikhs to the warrior caste. He introduced the Sikhs' practices of wearing Turbans and never cutting the hair and beard.

The Columbia Encyclopedia 3rd edition

There was a very good reason why the Guru had selected this symbol. Unshorn hairs had always been associated with saints and people who were regarded as "God's" chosen ones. Some historical persons wearing long hair were also believed to be possessed with supernatural powers. Guru Gobind Singh must have thought that by wearing long hair would clothe the Khalsa (pure or true Sikhs with a halo of holiness. Sikh historians state that Guru made it compulsory for the Khalsa to wear unshorn hair because their appearance, with beard and Turbans, made them conspicuous, and worthy of distinction and respect

**Teja Singh, formally Prof. of history
Khalsa College Amritsar**

Guru Gobind Singh made Sikhism more formal. He forbade smoking and cutting of hair at any period of life,

Encyclopedia of religion & ethics

The head priest of the Golden Temple and the Jathedar of Sri Akai Takhat (highest seat of authority Amritsar, are of the opinion that under no circumstances should a Sikh wear a cap or hat.

S. G. P. C.

The Sikh is inseparable from his Turbans. However foolish it may look to others. To a Sikh its essential mark of belonging to his faith and community. The British army recognized it as a permissible alternative to other prescribed head dresses.

Rev, J. Whittaker. M. A. St Agnes church Rusholme M/c

The ban on Sikh's wearing Turbans while employed on the buses should be rescinded because I believe this is a clear case of religious discrimination. I am sure that all religions can help to preserve the moral standards of the nation and help forward the living standards and good relationships between all citizens.

Rev. D. W. Quinn M.A. St. Mark's rectory, higher broughton Salford

The Sikh Turbans would have been colorful and attractive and would have given some emphasis to the fact that as a nation today we in England represent many races and many people.

Rev. L.H. Rhodes, vicar the vicarage, Urmston M/c

The question of cap being an absolutely necessary part of the regulation uniform hardly seems to stand examination when the cases of Sikhs in the armed forces, is considered. Mr. Kuljet Singh, a Turbaned Sikh, served in the RAF wearing Turbans as part of his uniform. In 1955 a young British service man became a Sikh: while abroad in the army he was allowed to keep the Turbans for the remainder of his service. If a Sikh can die in our forces with Turbans as part of his uniform why not also in our public services the maintenance of uncut hair is as important to a Sikh as is the avoidance of Port to a Jew, or Moslem.

Mrs. P. M. Wylam,
Editor of Sikh courier

The Sikh and his Turban

To The Editor of Manchester Guardian 3 July 1959
Sir the refusal of Manchester's Transport Committee to allow Sagar Singh to become a bus conductor unless he doffs his Turbans and dons a peaked cap is ridiculous. No organization can be much more hidebound with uniform regulations than the British army, but soldiers of Sikh faith in the colonies are allowed to wear their Turbans, surmounted by their regimental badges.

In Singapore Sikhs can be seen as Soldiers, Policemen, Bus drivers, Conductors and inspectors, all with Turbans and one might add, looking much smarter than other uniformed personnel in greasy peaked caps. Perhaps the Transport Committee is afraid that Sagar Singh will frighten old ladies off the Buses?

Yours & c.
Gerald R. Haigh

Said Gilbert Harding in the Sunday people 14/8/1960

How on earth can the hard headed, sensible people of Manchester put up with the interminable and fantastic argument that is wasting the time of their Corporation Transport Committee It is a simple matter.

A year ago a Sikh Gyani Sunder Singh, applied for a Conductors job on a Manchester buses. Everything about was perfectly acceptable except one thing. Being a Sikh, he was bound by his religion to wear Turbans whereas according to the Committees chairman councilor Morris: It has been a condition of the employment that drivers and conductors must wear a uniformed cap.

Sunder Singh Sagar promised that, not only would he be prepared to wear dark blue Turbans to match his uniform, but also on it he would wear the Corporation transport badge. No cap, No job.

Now seven leaders of the Sikh community in Manchester there are now about 700 of them have pleaded the Turbans case with chairman. He will pass on their plea to the committee; they will pass on their recommendation to the City Council. What a footling waste of people's time. The queen appears to have no objections at all to Sikhs wearing Turbans with her uniform. Why in sanity's name, should Manchester Corporation think their transport uniform more exclusive?

The Sikh's Turbans-Guardian 17/8/1960

To the Editor of the Guardian

Sir, I was distressed and astonished to learn that Manchester Corporation had forbidden the wearing of Turbans by bus drivers and conductors. This strange prohibition admittedly cannot be called political or racial discrimination. It is, however an extremely unpleasant example of religious discrimination, directed against people of particular faith -Sikh's.

Many groups of Indians who in the past wore Turbans have long since given them up. For them the Turbans was simply one kind of headgear among others, as it is to us. To the Sikh, however, the Turbans is a part of his religion, and no true Sikh will give up wearing it, even to secure a job with the Manchester Corporation.

The Indian army, Navy, and air force are as devoted to uniform smartness as are the British. But the Sikh was allowed to retain their Turbans. They were allowed to do so in the British period, and I am not aware that discipline or appearance suffered. Does the Manchester Corporation intend to maintain a religious discrimination against one particular group, and demonstrate to the world that it is less enlightened than ever the British Raj was in India?

If the Manchester Corporation really does wish expressly to exclude the Sikhs, that is a different matter. It will lose the services of some of the best drivers in the world.

Rev. R. H. S. Boyd, Belfast 9
NOTE: Turbaned Sikhs won the world's toughest car rally,
The East African Safari: Daily Mirror 20/11/1965

Times weekly, Atlantic edition, August 29th 1960

700 fellow Sikh's in Manchester drew up a document pointing out that in two world wars, 82,000 Turbaned Sikhs had been killed in battle and Sikh had won more than half of the Victoria Crosses awarded to the Indian army. If they died for Britain in their Turbans asked the Sikhs, could they not be allowed to work in them? Support also came from mighty Manchester Guardian: an editorial suggested that, with or without caps, no one looked tackier than the average Manchester bus conductor. Asked an indignant letter writer:

"If a man is clean, polite and has a sense of duty, what difference does a hat make? Unless, of course he is on the transport committee, and requires a hole in the head to talk through".

Discrimination the Guardian 3/10/1960

The Manchester City Council yesterday persisted in its refusal to allow Sikhs to wear Turbans as bus conductors. Their religion forbids them to appear in public without Turbans.

So rejecting another opportunity to redeem its reputation, the decision will be read about and wondered at not only in Britain. Reason advanced for this intolerance, there is little point in calling it anything else.

Turbans trouble Manchester Evening News 21/10/1960

The Manchester liberal Municipal committee strongly disapproved of the refusal of the City Transport Department to employ Sikhs as bus conductors and allow them to wear their Turbans, which have a sacred significance to them.

It is complete nonsense for Councilor Morris, the chairman, to say there is no objection to the employment of Sikhs so long as they do not wear their Turbans while on duty.

He must know that this is in effect, saying, "We will not employ Sikhs". The committee does not insist on their present staff wearing uniformed hats, many of them wear no hats at all on duty, so why this special reservation in the case of small numbers of Sikhs who might be concerned.

G. Phillip Robinson Manchester Liberal Federation

City Urged to review ban on Turbans Guardian December 1960

Mr. Edward Newbold, secretary of the Manchester and Salford Trades Council Suggested that Sikhs be allowed to wear blue Turbans with corporation official badge on it at a meeting of the trades' council last night, it represents 200,000 trade unionists, a motion deploring the corporations attitude was carried in principle. "I think blue Turbans with a cap badge would be equally as good as peaked cap".

The Guardian 10th January 1963

Alderman Sir Richard Harper, leader of the Conservative Party who argued that, while none of the committee members had advocated racial, religious discrimination in rejecting Turbans, this was the effect of their decision. It was like the man who said, "I did not kill him, I only moved the ladder".

Summary of Turbaned Sikhs' military services and sacrifices- For Britain and world freedom
The call to arms

We welcome here and greet the representative of India and first Maharaja of Patiala, the ruler who has inherited a tradition of attachment to the British crown and empire and worthily has filled the great tradition. His gallant people have not for the first time, fought side by side in this war with British troops in the battlefields. British soldiers welcome them as worthy comrades in arms.

Mr. Lloyd George, then Prime Minister of England spoke these words at the Empire Parliamentary Association Supper at the House of Lords on June 21st 1918 - From the book Patiala and the Great War

Who were the worthy comrades? These were Turbaned Sikh soldiers of Maharaja Patiala who fought on every front in the First World War and endured shellfire with no other protection but Turbans.

At their return to India, they were given official welcome at Karachi. Addressing the troops in Urdu on behalf of the army welcome committee

Mr. H.S. Lawrence, commissioner in Sindh, said:

"On behalf of the people of Hindustan (India we welcome you back on your safe return to your native country. The fame of the Indian cavalry was well known before the time of this Great War, but its fame has been increased a hundred folds by the brave deeds of daring endurance, that which you have performed during this war.

The conditions of this war have been beyond all previous experience and precedent, and cavalry have been required to perform duties for which they were not especially trained, but on no occasion have they been known to fail in performing their duties steadfastly and heroically".

We learn that you took part in the great campaigns, which protected Egypt and which conquered Mesopotamia, The manner in which Indian cavalry by their endurance in long marches not less by their skill in battle, won the full fruits of victory, has aroused admiration among armies of all nations. You have helped to preserve peace and happiness.

Patiala and the Great War
Thanks of British Government

Lt Governor of Punjab said at Patiala in February 1919, at the parade of Patiala Imperial services troops; "the Patiala Imperial Service troops were among the first to take the field against the enemy and you did not leave the field until the enemy was completely crushed.

You have worthily upheld the splendid tradition of the Patiala State and the Sikh race. The Infantry has done gallant service in Gallipoli, in the defense of Egypt, in the battle of Gaza.

In the arduous operation against Es-Sult and Maan, for which they received special praises from General Allenby, and in the final attack of September and October which led to the complete rout and surrender of Turkish Army". The cavalry played their part in the defense of Egypt at a critical stage and their services in Mesopotamia earned commendation of generals Maude and Marshall. I again thank you on behalf of the British government and wish you a long enjoyment of the glorious peace you have helped to earn.

Patiala and the Great War

"No one has fought more loyally and gallantly for us than Sikhs".

The Sikhs by Sir John J.H. Gardner KCB

"The contribution of the Sikh community in men and material was ten times that of any other community of India".

The great war 1914-18 by Sir John Maynard

The Sikh regiment in the Second World War
By Colonel F. T. Birdwood OBE

Five hundred pages of this book are full of bravery and glory of Sikhs who fought wearing Turbans only on their heads. Here is mentioned only the forward by General Sir Frank Messervy KCSI, KBE, CB, DSO.

It is great honor to me to have been asked to write this forward to the history of the Sikh regiments in the Second World War. As I read the proud story of the exploits of various battalions, so well presented in the book, many memories arise of those, which it was my good fortune to have under my command.

There was the 4th battalion in Eritrea with Gazelle force, and again in the western desert with the 4th Indian division.

Always ready for anything, cheerful surmounting the greatest difficulties and dangers, companies staunchly lying dug in while German tanks ran over them, but still there to deal with any infantry that might follow.

Then the last battalion in Burma and Malaya, always magnificent in and out of action, a unit to which one could give the severest task knowing that it would be done. As I recall their many fine actions, that first of all battle cry: "Jo Bole So Nihal Sat Siri Akal". (He who speaks that God is true will find happiness rings in my ears.

Except for machine gun battalion in Burma in 1944, this upheld the high traditions of the regiment. I did not serve with any of the ten battalions. But as one reads, a Great Spirit of a great regiment shining bright and clear in places overcoming every doubt inspires one. Exultant in hard won victory, undimmed in adversity; in fine achievement and victory as 2nd battalion in Iraq, Persia, in the western desert and Italy; in defeat and disaster as the 5thth battalion in Malaya, yet still fighting undaunted to the end.

In less glorious but essential duty of keeping peace in Persia and Iraq Yet never losing efficiency; as the 3rd battalion in the enthusiastic training of all reinforcements for Burma. As the 14th battalion in keeping watch and ward on the frontier of India; as the 6th and 7th and 15th battalions; as infantry turned gunners in the 8th and 9th battalions; in monotonous but necessary garrison duties, as the 26ü' battalion.

"FINALLY WE THAT LIVE ON CAN NEVER FORGET THOSE COMRADES WHO IN GIVING THEIR LIVES GAVE SO MUCH THAT IS GREAT AND GOOD TO THE STORY OF THE SIKH REGIMENT. NO LIVING GLORY CAN TRANCEND THAT OF THEIR SUPREME SACRIFICE. THEY REST IN PEACE".

During the First World War in the British Indian army, 904 Indian officers and 61.052 other ranks lost their lives, a total of 61.956; 1680 Indian officers, 10812 other Indian ranks, a total of 1070 reported prisoners of war.

Statistics taken from efforts of British Empire during the Great War 914-20 page 237

In British Indian army in First World War 75% of Turbans-wearing Sikhs were involved in battle. According to this ratio, 46542 Turbans wearing Sikhs were killed in action and 50166 were wounded, 8301 were prisoners of war.

During the Second World War in the British Indian army, 48.674 were killed in action. 65.174 were wounded and great total were unknown.

Figures from summary of casualties-Second World War 1939-1945 table 14 page 111 from the book This war Business by A.G. Enoch 1951)

According to the ratio 75% of Turbans wearing Sikhs were killed, 58.879 were wounded and the great total for both wars' 83.055 Turbans wearing Sikhs killed 109.045 Turbans wearing Sikhs were wounded. They died, or wounded for the freedom of Britain and the world. Enduring shellfire with no other protection but their Turbans the symbol of their faith

Mr. Ram Singh, a Bhatra Sikh wore Turbans during his service with the A. R. P. in Birmingham in the Second World War. After the blitz, when the late king George VI toured Birmingham, the Turbans of Ram Singh Bhatra drew the attention of the King, and the King spoke to Mr. Ram Singh (a photo was published in the daily mirror, 12th Dec 1940)

Mr. Ram Singh Bhatra was my religious colleague and we are members of most religious minded Bhatra Sikh tribe. The Bhatra Sikhs were among the first to come to this country in the early 40s and ever since they came they have been very successful in keeping their self identity and their Sikh faith alive by keeping their Sikh symbol of the Turbans on

They were the first Sikh tribe to make the very first Post-war Sikh Temple in Manchester and later two more. Master Tara Singh, the Indian Sikh leader who visited the Sikh Temple, publicly praised their religious devotion. Each and every town where the Bhatra Sikhs are living they have Sikh Temple and some town have two or three of them. At present time the Bhatra Sikhs have about 40/50 temples in the UK

Views of Ex-Soldiers

Dear Mr. Sagar.

With reference to your letter excellent letter of today in the paper, I feel I must write to tell you how much I agree with you and your countrymen in this disgraceful subject. When the public services of' Great City give priority to non-British subjects over the Sikh community because of the wearing of a Turbans, which has a religious significance, I feel strongly that that is a denial of freedom.

In the last war I served in the king's own royal regiment in INDIA, Iran and Libya alongside the 2/11 Sikhs in the 25th Indian infantry brigade, and I can say in an honesty I never served with a better men anywhere. Their loyalty, courage, and comradeship was something to be seen also when I was wounded and taken prisoner, I found their steadfastness in captivity was a credit to your great race.

In prison camps in Italy, I made firm friends with many Sikhs. I assure you I would feel proud to have my bus ticket given to me by a Sikh. All best wishes to you in any campaign you may have in the future for freedom of employment anywhere. The British Commonwealth owes a great debt to you all.

Yours very sincerely Clifford Walton Blood

Manchester Evening News 24/3/1966

"I am sure I am speaking on behalf of thousands of servicemen who knew the Sikhs in the North Africa. Let Manchester show a magnificent gesture to these wonderful men by honoring them to allow them to Turbans under which they served Britain so faithfully".

William Chapman
Levenshulme Manchester

The Turbans

"If English officers could serve in the Sikh regiment in the Indian army without beard and with caps, why cannot Sikhs serve here with beard and Turbans? Wherever there are old army officers in charge, they would not hesitate to take Sikhs in any service.

Capt. Gurdial Singh, Manchester

From Julian S. Goldstone
Councilor City Council Manchester

The Sikh fought with our army in two wars and they endured shellfire with no other protection but the Turbans because of the intensity of their faith. If we were prepared to allow them to fight for us wearing the Turbans, surely they can serve us on our buses similarly clad. Queen Victoria always had a Turbaned Sikhs as her bodyguard.

From Dr. S.S. Chatterjee MB M.R.C.P. (London,)
President Indian Association Manchester

Turbans are part of Sikh religion. In fact it is more than a way of life. From the very day of its adoption as part of Sikh religion it has been accepted as smart piece of headgear, if not the smartest of all the male headgear. The viceroys of India always had Turbans as favored uniforms for their bodyguards.

From Russell E. Talbot
Hon secretary Indian League Lancashire

During my 21 years membership of the India league, the last 18 of them as secretary of the Lancashire committee, I have enjoyed the close co-operation and friendship of many members of Manchester's Sikh community.

I know, therefore, how deeply and sincerely the majority of Sikhs regard their religion and its insignia. Which is indeed inseparable from the faith of the true Sikh? The most readi-

ly recognized symbol of Sikh religion are the Turbans and the beard, both integral part of the faith.

Those of us, who have other religious beliefs and claim right to practice our faith in accordance with our beliefs, cannot fail to extend the same rights, which we claim for ourselves to others. The Sikh community of Manchester has shown its great sense of civic responsibility and pride in being citizens of this great city, and there should be no barriers in the way of their opportunities for service to the city and the people of Manchester- their fellow citizens.

Parliamentary support for Turbans
Mr. Frank Taylor MP

I have met many Sikhs, both in their homeland of India and Pakistan and also as immigrants here in England. In India, before the partition under the British rule, the Sikhs were regarded as perhaps the most reliable race in the whole of that vast country. Close bonds of friendship were forged right up to the day of partition, which have survived those trying days and continue right up to the present.

In England, we English look upon the Sikhs as tried friends, we recognize them as groups of closed knit communities throughout the country and we both recognize and respect their strong religious background. In particular, we respect and appreciate their wearing of the Turbans, not only because it's religious importance but because of its attractive appearance.

As is well known, I have fought against the Manchester city corporation to try to persuade them to permit Sikhs to wear their Turbans while employed on public transport and will continue to use whatever pressure I can to achieve this end. Certain other cities in England have given way on this point, and I hope one-day Manchester will follow them.

Mr. Taylor has fulfilled his pledge in putting the following motion to the House of Commons on 21.4.66, which has not yet been answered;

"Wearing of Turbans by Sikhs: that this house deplores the fact that the City of Manchester Corporation still refuses to acknowledge the religious significance of the Turbans to Sikhs, *and by prohibiting Sikhs from wearing these Turbans if employed on public transport, Effectively prevent devout Sikhs from filling posts which many of them are anxious to fill, and for which they are well suited".*

From Alderman Leslie Lever MP

I am opposed to all forms of intolerance. As the Sikh community regards the wearing of Turbans as part of their sacred faith, they should not be discriminated against on that account. I had the privilege of meeting them as lord mayor of Manchester and they are loyal and good citizens.

From Sir Robert Carey

I have fought alongside Sikhs in France in the First World War and later in Iraq and North Persia. Sikhs are wonderful race of people, much admired by me. I have written to the town clerk, Sir Philip Dingle, about the wearing of Turbans on duty on Corporation buses"

From Mr. Will Griffiths MP

I know Gyani Sagar and his colleagues in the Sikh community have been concerned for some years that some public authorities have refused to employee Sikhs who insist on wearing their Turbans. I have long believed that this was an objection, which barred them from making a useful contribution to the British economy.

I have noted that some government departments have now dropped their objection. I hope this will become general practice.

I served alongside Sikh soldiers with the 18th army in the western desert, and I know their religion makes it obligatory to wearing the Turbans whilst on duty and never to uncover their sacred hair. I hope that their campaign will be a universal successful.

From Mr. Stanley Orem MP

The Sikhs in Britain and particularly in Manchester have a long outstanding record of Operation with the British people.

I am of the firm opinion that they should be allowed to wear their national and religious head-dress-Turbans-at work or at any other time

Therefore these ridiculous impositions placed on their employment by certain employers are quite unwarranted and must definitely support the stand taken by Gyani Sagar on behalf of the Sikh community in this country.

From Mr. N.H. Lever MP

I would, in the circumstances, make it possible for Sikhs to observe their own religious faith without debarring them from public services in this way. It seems that other local authorities have found this possible, and I would have hoped that the Manchester Corporation, too, would follow suit. I have written to the lord mayor of Manchester, sending him a copy of this correspondence.

From Mr. K. Zilliacus MP

I have long known that for Sikh community is virtually an article of religion not to cut their hair or beard and of course the wearing of Turbans follows from that rule.

Mr. Clever MP for Yardley Birmingham

Asked the minister of labor if he would introduce a legislation to ensure that employees should not be debarred under their terms of employment from wearing clothes with religious significance for them

Mr. Hare minister for labor ' I do not think legislation would be appropriate. I am sure it is better that occasional difficulties should be settled by common sense and understanding between the parties concerned".

Mr. Clever In view of the fact Turbans wearing Sikhs fought alongside our men with gallantry during the last war, during which 36.000 were killed and 58.000 wounded, would not my right Hon friend consider it rather pity to prevent Sikhs wearing Turbans when issuing tickets on buses".

Mr. Hare "I think this is a matter which is better settled by negotiations and discussions with parties concerned. If we were to get into legislation, defining variations of religious dress, religious holidays and so on, we would be getting into a lot of trouble".

Why trouble in case of Turbans? It seems that the ministers have not seen the editorial of the Guardian of 11th August 1960.

It has been suggested that to admit Turbans would be to open the gate to all sorts of eccentricities in dress. To that there are two short answers. First, Newcastle-upon-Tyne has engaged six Sikh bus conductors and has had no trouble whatever in maintaining its sartorial standards since. Secondly, there are few garments, which can claim the religious sanctions of a Sikh Turbans. And most of those rule themselves out by purely practical considerations; for example an afghan lady wishing to act as a conductor in a Burka, if that is conceivable, would have difficulty in climbing the stairs.

The Sikh's Turbans is practical, small, and well defined, and Sikhs are in general noted for their fine bearing. Let them in and not only in Manchester and Newcastle" moreover, the Sikh representatives, under my leadership, who met the chairman of the transport committee, and general manager, together with interested members of the city council.

At 55 Piccadilly, on 10.8.1960 assured the transport committee that Sikhs would wear Turbans of any color chosen by the Manchester Corporation Transport Department, with corporation badge on it, and will supply their own Turbans. They would work on any day they would be asked to work.

During the struggle for Turbans of Mr. Amar Singh with London transport which has now accepted that Mr. Amar Singh can wear Turbans with uniform, one reader wrote in the Daily Express of 15.9.64. "Had members of London transport management spent several years in the western descent".

The sights of Turbans at that time would have gladdened their hearts. It was a symbol of stout, fearless-comrades-in-arms, which should not be forgotten.

From Alderman Sir Richard Harper Kt. JP

To whom it may concern — for upwards often years I have been privileged to make frequent contact with members of Manchester Sikh community generally, and with Gyani S.S. Sagar in particular. 1 have always found the "Wearers of Turbans" to be honest, loyal, industrious and of high moral integrity. I am wholly behind them in their desire to wear the symbol of their religion and race-the Turbans.

From Julian S. Goldstone Councilor City Council Manchester

The Sikh fought with our army in two wars and they endured shellfire with no other protection but the Turbans because of the intensity of their faith. If we were prepared to allow them to fight for us wearing the Turbans, surely they can serve us on our buses similarly clad. Queen Victoria always had a Turbaned Sikhs as her bodyguard.

The seemingly impossible becomes possible

Members of House of Lords are entitled to become members of the House of Commons if they wish. The archbishop of Canterbury meets his holiness the pope in Rome. Ladies may wear hats in the House of Lords, but Sikhs of Manchester cannot wear Turbans on the buses while up to now Newcastle-upon-Tyne, Birmingham, Bristol, Glasgow, London transport, GPO, British

Railways and British army have accepted the rights of Sikhs to wear the Turbans with uniform.

The Ex-chairman of Manchester Transport Committee Mr. C.R. Morris who is now MP for Openshawe writes in reply to my letter, that if the above circumstances of acceptance of Turbans by the other authorities had been known before, it might influence the Manchester corporation transport Committee.

He agrees with the view expressed by Alderman Langton, the Lord Mayor of the city of Manchester, that the question be re-submitted to the Manchester Corporation Transport Department. If, in the light of general acceptance, of Turbans in the country that Turbans being part of the Sikh religion

Manchester Corporation Transport Department Allows Sikhs to wear their Turbans whilst employed by the transport Department. It might not be too late to improve harmonious race relations in the City.

If Manchester Corporation Transport Department still keeps refusing Sikhs employment on public services due to Turbans, their attitude is nothing else but religious discrimination against Sikhs, which worse than racial discrimination.

The liberal assembly at Brighton in 1963 has left no doubt of their opinion of religious discrimination practiced against Sikhs by MCTD.

When Col. George Wigg. For Dudley successfully championed the campaign of Mr. Baldev Singh for long hair, beard and Turbans with Minister of Defense, at the end he commented "for six months he fought red tape and Nonsense".

Singh and his beard join up

Private Baldev Singh, with long hair and beard and Turbans joined the army yesterday keeping his religion and faith intact by order of the Minister of defense.

THE GREAT INJUSTICE

If a, minister of defense can step in for the benefit of a private soldier. Will the minister of labor, archbishop of Canterbury, and the lord Mayor of Manchester. Alderman B Langton Being members of race relations board) use their influence on behalf of Manchester Sikhs, Manchester Corporation should continue the ban on Turbans, or will they allows the reputation of Manchester to be less bright because of this great injustice of religious discrimination?

According to the views expressed by lord mayor Alderman B. Langton and the Indian High Commissioner Dr. Jivraj Mehta the following applications have been submitted to the chairman of Manchester Transport Department, to lift the ban on Turbans.

Gyani S. S. Sagar (Hon in Punjabi Language and Literature)
39, Morley Ave, Fallowfield, Manchester

To The Chairman
Manchester Corporation Transport Department

12 Devonshire Street
Ardwick
Manchester 12

Dear Sir
Since you last discussed the question of Sikhs wearing Tur-
bans with uniform being employed on your buses, more author-
ities have accepted the right of Sikhs to wear Turbans with uni-
form. Up to now, Newcastle-upon-Tyne, Birmingham, Bristol,
Huddersfield, London Transport, Glasgow, GPO, British Rail-
ways and the British Army have allowed Sikh to wear Turbans
with their uniforms as symbol of their faith.

In the light of general acceptance of Turbans being accepted
in the country, as part of Sikh religion and the new feeling of
harmonious relationship in the city, we approach you on behalf
of the Sikhs of Manchester to reconsider your previous decision.
Thanking you
yours faithfully

Gyani S. S. SAGAR Religious advisor

This pamphlet is edited by:
Gyani Sundar Singh Sagar
Hon in Punjabi Language & Literature (Punjab University) Past
president, Sarab Hind Bhatra Union of India, now religious advisor to
all three Sikh Temples published this pamphlet

The members who presented the application were:
Bhai Mehar Singh Pardesi (Sikh Priest)
Guru Nanak Nirankari Gurdwara
15 Monton Street, Moss Side, Manchester 14
Sewa Singh Himat
General Secretary
 Guru Nanak Nirankari Gurdwara
15 Monton Street, Moss Side, Manchester 14
Pritam Singh Rasila
General Secretary

Sikh Temple and Mission Centre
35 Rosamund Street, Chorlton –on- Medlock, Manchester 13
Shingar Singh Sangi
General Secretary
Deshmesh Sikh Temple
Halliwell Lane Cheetham hill, Manchester 8
  Cc: Rt. Worshipful Lord Mayor of Manchester, Rt. Rev. Dean of Manchester

After producing this dossier and presenting it to the transport committee, they still were reluctant to give way to Sikh being employed on their buses. But the determination and support of the Sikh community and local councilors and former military personnel who had served in the British Indian army during the world wars, with the Sikh regiments, a petition was presented to the rightful Lord Mayor of Manchester out lining the discrimination towards Sikhs. Due to pressure from their own councilors, public and the other towns who already had Sikh employees on their city buses, the transport Committee succumbed hold a meeting with community leaders at their head quarters in Manchester Piccadilly

Meeting of the transport committee on Wednesday 10th August 1960 And Sewak Jatha of Sikh Temples Manchester 14

Ref: C268/60/FU

statement

1. After debate in July 1959, to discuss the employment of Sikhs, wearing Turbans, on the Manchester Corporation Buses, the opinions of the Manchester people and other parts of the country reported in the newspapers showed a general feeling in favour of employing the Sikhs wearing Turbans on the buses. The transport committee has ignored those opinions by continuing to refuse employment to Sikhs who wear Turbans.

2. We have lived in Manchester for a long time and have made it our permanent home. The people of Manchester have been most

helpful and have accepted us with friendliness into their community, and we are indeed most grateful to them. Our children attend your schools, wearing Turbans, along with your children and are happily accepted, but why shouldn't they be.

They enjoy equal facilities with your children, are equally well educated, well supplied and well looked after. Later then, should they attend for employment to your department, will the door be closed in their face because they wear Turbans. If so this is morally wrong and injustice. The Turbans to which you so much object is " part and parcel" of a proper Sikh's life; the life which Sikhs have spent among the British people, here and abroad, for more than Century

3. The right of the Turbans was accepted in the British Indian forces where the question of uniform is more important than bus uniform and was allowed to be worn with the rest of the military apparel.

We should remind you of the sacrifices that Turbaned Sikhs made in the cause of freedom. During the First World War in the British Indian army 904 Indian officers, and 61.052 in other ranks lost their lives; a total of 62.056, 1.680 Indian officers, 62.209 other ranks a total of 66.889 wounded, of which 258 Indian officers 10.812 other ranks a total of 11.070 reported prisoners of war.

In the British Indian army approximately 75% consisted of Turbans wearing Sikhs, according to this ratio: 46.542 Turbans Sikhs were killed; 50.166 wounded; 8.301 were made prisoners of war; these figures were taken from "statistics of military effort of the British Empire during the great war of 1914-1920, page 237"

During the Second World War, in the British Indian army, 48.674 were killed; 65.174 were wounded; total prisoners unknown. According to the ration 75% consisted of Turbans wearing Sikhs. 36.513 Turbans wearing Sikhs were killed and 58.879 were wounded; figures taken from: - "summary of casualties in the second world war, 1939-1945, table 14 page 111 from the book "This war Business" by A.G. Enoch published 1951.

Sikhs even wore Turbans in the parachute operations, most dangerous operations during the war. More than half of the Victoria crosses which were awarded to the British Indian armies were won by Turbans wearing Sikhs. Had these men not fought along with your men and died for freedom, we shall not now all be enjoying such happy state of affairs. So we, who fought side by side with your own forces, are now being refused equality of employment with your department, because of the same Turbans we wore in the war. If we could die with it, we have every right to live and work with it.

4. It is usually said that what Manchester does today the rest of the country does tomorrow, but in this case we have fallen short because Newcastle has done it first. With due respect and thanks to Councillor Trevor Thomas, with his given consent, I shall read a letter which was received from Newcastle upon Tyne transport department, which relates to the present position. After hearing what Newcastle has to say, your refusal to allow employment to Sikhs who wear Turbans is even more mystifying, because the public in Newcastle cannot be any different from the public in Manchester.

Newcastle Corporation Transport & Electricity Undertaking
25th July 1960
Councillor Trevor Thomas
21 Gate Street
Openshawe
Manchester 11

<u>Employment of Sikhs wearing Turbans</u>

Dear Sir,

Thank you for your letter of 23rd July, and I would inform you that no variations from standard uniforms are allowed except in the case of Sikhs who are permitted, on religious grounds to wear a blue Turban in place of the uniform cap. The Turban is dark blue to blend with the uniform and there are six Sikhs employed and they have carried out their duties satisfactorily

We should very much like to clarify the position regarding the five "Ks" referred to in the last meeting, and explained in a previous letter, and to stress that it is impossible for any of these to effect or hinder a Sikh when carrying out his duties.

We feel that some explanation is due to us with regard to the rules; we feel that these are old and out dated. When they were first made, the chance of a Sikh wearing Turbans applying for a job was very slight, but times have changed, and there are many hundreds of Sikhs in Manchester area, so we feel that some amendment should be made to coincide with these changes. We emphasise that our Turbans are respected in all the British Crown Courts, and the American government has recently allowed Sikhs wearing Turbans in their defence force, as quoted in the Manchester Guardian on 4/8/1959.

We reaffirm that if you reconsider your decision and decide in our favour, every Sikh applying for a post will give you a written guarantee, that he will supply his own Turbans, either navy blue to blend with the uniform or a colour to be chosen by MCTD. We request that you reconsider with sympathy and feeling of brotherliness towards our commonwealth people who have become the citizens of Manchester. We feel that the Turbans will add beauty and colour to the commonwealth scene here, and what we are asking may bring "wind of change" in bus services in Manchester, and it would probably bring more passengers to see how hard and well we work.

Yours faithfully

General Manager

Memorandum of Meeting of the Manchester Corporation Transport Department
Ref: C.260/60/LC

Memorandum of meeting between the chairman of the Transport Committee and General Manager, together with other interested members of the City Council and representatives of the Sikh Community, held at 55 Piccadilly Manchester on Wednesday the 10th August 1960

Present:
Council Members and Officials
Councillor C. R. Morris (Chair, Transport Committee)
Alderman Sir Richard Harper
Councillor Trevor Thomas
Councillor F. P. Evans
Councillor C. O. Sanders

Mr. A. F. Neal (General Manager)

Mr. E. H. Stiff (Secretary)

Mr. J. F. J. Webb (personnel Officer)

Deputation from the Sikh Community:

Mr. B.M. Singh (President)

Mr. Mela Singh (Vice-President)

Mr. Kalyan Singh (General Secretary)

Mr. M. S. Pardesi (Priest)

Mr. Jarnail Singh (cashier)

Mr. Gyani Sundar Singh Sagar (Religious Advisor and Spokesperson)

Mr. B.S. Rattan (former general Secretary)

The meeting commenced at 10.15am and the Chairman of the Transport Committee, Councillor C. R. Morris welcomed all members to the meeting.

Councillor Morris mentioned that he had a series of questions which he would ask the Sikhs to answer; but first invited them to state their case. He explained that the question of the issue as to whether the transport undertaking of Manchester would permit members of the platform staff to wear Turban is not based in any respect on religious discrimination.

Mr. Gyani Sundar Singh Sagar, who was the Sikh who originally applied for employment in the department as a bus conductor last year, was the spokesman for the deputation and he read the attached statement.

Questions were then put to Mr. Sagar by the chairman, Councillor C.R. Morris, and the General Manager, as follows:-

Question

Is the Turban national head-dress?

Answer

The cap is not national head dress, but the Turban can be called National head dress, but is also of religious significance. Sikhs never take off their turbans whilst taking food, and they never wear a cap.

Question

Is the wearing of Turban demanded by the Sikh religion?

Answer

Yes if he is a "proper" Sikh.

Question

Does this apply to all Sikhs, or certain sects or groups?

Answer

It applies to all "proper" Sikhs.

Question

Presumably as with other religions, some members strictly observe the rules and customs, and some are not so particular. Is it realised that the members of other religious sects, who strictly adhere to their principles, are also unable to undertake conducting and driving for the department? (Orthodox Jews, Jehovah's Witnesses , Seventh day Adventists)

The orthodox Jews obliged not to work on Saturdays. The Sikhs are aware of this fact, but wearing of a Turban was part of their dress and would not interfere with the working of any particular day and was simply a substitution for the uniform cap.

Question

Are Sikhs allowed to wear turbans in any other uniformed services other than Army?

Answer

It was appreciated that no Sikhs wearing turbans were employed in other services, e.g. G.P.O. but could not state defiantly that this was so. Manchester transport undertaking is public service, and because of this the Sikhs have right to be employed. If public services will not have Sikhs, people will think there is something wrong with them, and this will gradually affect their living. It is not only a question of this refusal gradually affecting our living, but we cannot accept that it is anything but religious discrimination since we make our appeal on religious grounds, conscience bond between our faith and God.

Question

In the Army itself are not Sikhs usually in self-contained units, battalions, regiments, companies, squadrons? Is there any difference between kilted Scotsman for example and Sikhs in this regard?

Answer

There are kilted regiments, but Scotsman does not wear kilts in other units?

Question

Do not other Indians regard Turban as important?

Answer

The Sikhs have worked with other regiments and battalions and not in just separate units. Scotsman do not wear kilts in general employment in Scotland, but Sikhs always do wear turbans all over the world. The kilt is not part of a Scotsman's religion, but just his national dress.

Question

Do they not agree that in an undertaking like Manchester, all sections of men should be treated equally? Why do they contend that Sikhs particularly should have special treatment which is not granted to other religions and sects?

Answer

The Sikhs do not agree to special concessions being asked for or given to them. The Turban is merely a replacement of the cap and not something additional. The Sikhs will still be wearing headgear.

Question

The undertaking employs men of many races, including over 100 men from India, Pakistan, Africa and West Indies as drivers and conductors, and a further 35 in the depots. None of these men are demanding special considerations?

Answer

The Sikhs appreciate the point mentioned, but if they agree, discrimination is being made against them because of their religion and beliefs in wearing turbans.

Question

Are Sikhs able to get any special dispensation in relation to the Turban, e.g. wear a token Turban?

Answer

As far as dispensation being granted is concerned, no concession is being asked for but just acceptance of the Turban instead of the cap. There are other aspects of the religion apart from the wearing of turbans, but

Sikhs are prepared to accept those; it is just the wearing of the turbans which is in dispute.

Question

Would they confirm that they knew that there was no objection to Sikhs with turbans working in the garages, and that the only point at issue is that undertaking considers that when men are employed as conductors, the standard uniform cap should be worn?

Answer

They resented the attitude that Sikhs were only suitable for working the garages such as washing buses, and not suitable to be employed as drivers and conductors.

Question

What is the difference between "proper Sikh" and "other" Sikhs?
A "proper Sikh" is bound to keep his hair and beard and to wear a Turban at all times. "Other Sikhs" who have cut their hair and shaved their beard and removed the Turban are those who have sinned against their religion.

Question

Would there be any objections to working any special days e.g. holy days?

Answer

It was not part of their religion to have certain holy days off, it would not interfere with working of the department. They are prepared to work all days they asked of them.

Question

As other religious adherents have special rules and customs, which prevent their working for M.C.T.D. how could special concessions for the Sikhs be justified?

Answer

They appreciated this and they had more religious customs apart from the wearing of turbans, but the wearing of the Turban was the only custom which they asked to be observed, and this would not in any way interfere with working of the department.

Question

With reference to the comb produced by Mr. Sagar and which carried the token dagger and avoided the need to carry a dagger – was it not possible for some form of token Turban to be worn, as it was understood that the covering of the hair was part of their religion, and wearing the ordinary uniform cap would do this? One Indian with long hair and beard in the department does wear the uniform cap.

A

Small changes have been made over the years, but wearing of the Turban had in fact, been in force for five hundred years. On the other hand, the dagger had only been in use for two hundred and fifty years-comparatively modern. The changing of the rule regarding the wearing of turbans would be major change, and at the moment this had not been done. Mr. Sagar emphasised again that they were not asking for a concession as such, merely the acceptance of the Turban instead of the cap. This would still be head-gear which apparently was the point the department insisted upon. Mentioned was made that all conductors do not wear caps whilst working, whereas they would always wear their head-gear. They had right to vote in this country and also to buy property, and yet they are being denied use of their Turban in certain employment. There was no freedom if they are to be told they can only work in garages, but they are not suitable to work on the buses themselves. During the war, for reasons of necessity, the rules were amended to allow women to be employed o the buses, why now then cannot the rules be relaxed because of demand and necessity.

B

Mr. Sagar produced a letter from the High Commission of India, regarding the national head-dress. This was perused by the Chair, Councillor C.R. Morris, and other members of the deputation. Members of the committee were asked if they had any questions to ask but they said no further questions were required.

C

In conclusion, Mr. Sagar made a plea regarding the bar in certain employment which is being enforced. He said it gave Sikhs a feeling of inferiority, if they are only to be allowed to in the garages and not on the buses. Women are employed by certain undertakings, and this meant that the Sikhs were considered by Manchester not to be as good as women, although women were not employed now on Manchester buses. The principle of inferiority, however, still remained.

D

Councillor Morris then said that the views of the Sikhs and the answers to the questions would be placed before the September 1960 meeting of the transport committee. Their decision would be put before the city council at their meeting in October 1960

E

Mr. Sagar then expressed his thanks on behalf of the deputation for the attendance of the councillors and for their consideration.

F

Councillor Morris asked if he could be left with a copy of the statement which was produced by Mr. Sagar when he first rose to speak to the deputation, and Mr. Sagar said he would leave this copy with the committee.

Finally on 18th October 1960 during the meeting held at General offices

Of the Manchester Corporation Transport Committee 55 Piccadilly Manchester 1

Ref –G4

All communications to be addressed to the General Manager.

Manchester Corporation Transport Department.

General Offices 55, Piccadilly.

Manchester, 1.

A. F. NEAL. B. SC. (ENG.).
A.M.I.E.E., M. INST. T..
GENERAL MANAGER

TELEPHONE NO. 2122 CENTRAL.
TELEGRAMS: CIVICBUSES, MANCHESTER.

IN REPLY PLEASE QUOTE

OUR REF. G4/T/P.

YOUR REF.

18th October, 1960.

Mr. Kalyan Singh,
General Secretary,
Sewak Jatha of the Sikh Temple,
15, Monton Street,
Moss Side,
MANCHESTER.14.

Dear Sir,

Employment of Sikhs Wearing Turbans

I refer to your letter of the 26th August, 1960, suggesting certain alterations to the draft minutes of the meeting held in these offices on the 10th August, which I forwarded to you with my letter of the 17th August, and also to the statement which was made by your deputation at the meeting.

The amendments suggested by you were incorporated in the statement and in the minutes of the meeting, and I enclose a copy of the revised documents which were placed before the Transport Committee at its meeting today.

The Committee after giving this question very full and careful consideration and in particular the representations made by you, as set out in the enclosed minute and attached statement, adopted the following resolution —

"THAT this Committee approve of
the employment of men of any religious
belief whatsoever as platform staff
provided that they comply with the
Department's Conditions of Service
relating to staff."

Yours faithfully,

GENERAL MANAGER.

Enclosure

/AJ.

92

The Fight Goes On

Gyani Ji's fight for justice didn't end after his first battle. When the British government introduced the law that required all motorbike riders to wear crash helmets, Gyani Ji challenged it. Two Sikh motorbike riders were stopped by police in Gravesend for not wearing helmets, which led to the formation of the "National Turbans Action Committee UK," headed by Baldev Singh Chahal, and Gyani Ji was asked to lead the campaign. He immediately brought the issue to the attention of the media, and national and local press and TV ran extensive stories about the problems of wearing turbans while riding a motorcycle.

Gyani Ji argued that Sikhs had been allowed to lay down their lives for Britain during the Raj and two world wars without any legal compulsion to wear helmets, so they deserved the right to choose what to wear while riding a motorcycle. Simply putting turbans over helmets was not a solution, as it contravened the religious practice of wearing turbans. Changing a law is a slow process and requires continuous and effective campaigning. Despite being 57 and suffering from asthma and diabetes, Gyani Ji decided to commit himself completely to the cause at whatever personal cost. He bought a motorcycle and rode it proudly through Manchester, being stopped and arrested several times.

Manchester became the battleground for the right to wear turbans, and Gyani Ji's refusal to pay the fines because he did not recognize the validity of the law led him to be given custodial. He was not afraid of serving time in prison for his cause, and he believed that it would further highlight the arguments he was making through his many correspondences. However, before he could serve his seven-day sentence in Strange ways prison, his fines were paid by a sympathetic Lord Mayor who thought he was saving Gyani Ji from self-inflicted punishment but had, in fact, undone all his hard work. Undaunted, Gyani Ji repeated his acts and once again was sentenced and served seven days in Strange ways.

On the day of his release, he instructed his son to bring a moped to the prison gates. In front of the national and local press, TV, and radio, he was garlanded with flowers and amidst cheers of Sikhs and non-Sikh supporters, proceeded to ride his motorcycle home. He was accompanied by his supporters and, of course, the local constabulary.

He was stopped and booked seven times on his ride home that day and was ready for another venture more extended stay in prison. However, largely through Gyani Ji's efforts, an amendment to the law was making its way through parliament.

On 15th November 1976, "An Act to exempt Turban-wearing followers of the Sikh religion from wearing a crash helmet when riding a motor-cycle" was passed (Motor-Cycle Crash Helmet) (Religious Exemption Act 1976 Chapter 62, Section32, Road Traffic Act 1972). Gyani Ji saw this as something for everyone to be proud of and said that "while it was a great day for Sikhs, it was a victory for the people of this great country and common sense."

The Helmet-Case

In 1973, the British government passed a law requiring anyone riding a two-wheeler to wear a helmet. This law banned Sikhs wearing turbans from riding motorbikes. Gyani Sundar Singh Sagar did not agree and bought a moped, riding it without a helmet until he was stopped by the police and charged. Gyani Ji refused to pay the fine and was imprisoned for seven days at HP Strangeways Manchester.

On the day of his release, the media and the Sikh community gathered to welcome him back, and he was garlanded with flowers. To defy the law, he rode the moped again with media and community supporters present, making a point about the injustice against Sikhs riding motorbikes. This protest became known as the "Turbans-Helmet" case. While riding his moped home, he was charged seven times for not wearing a helmet.

Epilogue

This manuscript was produced by Gyani Sundar Singh Sagar as evidence of the Sikh religion and the sacrifices made during the two world wars with turbans intact. I am privileged to be able to reproduce this article from my late uncle who did so much for the Sikh community of Manchester. Later, in an exhibition at Central Library Manchester, his son Ujjal Didar Singh Sagar (Man for All People) exhibited the motorbike used by Gyani Ji.

The Manchester Smagam 2017

Every year, the Manchester council of five Gurdwaras organizes an annual procession of Nagar Kirtan through the city centre of Manchester, visiting each Gurdwara Sahib. The procession starts from a different Gurdwara Sahib each year, taking their turn starting at one and finishing at another. All the necessary permissions from various departments and authorities, such as police, traffic management, and the town hall in Albert Square, are obtained to organize the procession.

In 2017, the five Gurdwara council of Manchester decided to hold a three-day Kirtan-Smagam in Manchester, the first one in the North West of England. The organizing committee searched for a suitable venue that would accommodate a large gathering and decided to hold it in the grounds of the Education Academy adjacent to Guru Nanak Dev Ji Gurdwara Moss Side. The dates were 27th, 28th, and 29th July 2017, Friday, Saturday, and Sunday.

One large tent was erected for the main Diwan hall, and a small one for the Amrit-Sanchar. The academy allowed the use of their gym for Langar hall, and the preparation of Langar was done outside the building by the Sewadars. The Kabuli Sangat provided support in many ways during the three days.

The main Kirtan-Jatha came especially for the Smagam from India, and some local lecturers were also invited. To accommodate all the visitors, one full hall of student residence, consisting of 100 rooms, was rented by a devoted Sewadar. This was for the Sangat as well as the visitors from overseas.

The members and the Sangat of all five Gurdwaras took part in doing Sewa, and the Amrit-Sanchar took place on Sunday, the last day of the Smagam, in the small tent that was specially erected for this purpose. During the three days, medical cover was provided by doctors and nurses working in the nearby Manchester Royal Infirmary hospital. St. John's Ambulance service and first aid were also in attendance all three days. Many other organizations, such as the police, fire brigade, and St. John's Ambulance service, were invited to have their training and recruitment workshops, and many learned life-saving skills.

The three-day event was very successful, thanks to the efforts of all the Manchester Sikh Sangat who worked tirelessly in organizing and managing it, making it a successful event to be remembered forever. The solidarity of the five Gurdwaras was praised by many prominent Kirtan-Jatha who took part in the three-day event.

.

Mukhtiar Singh Pardesi

Mukhtiar Singh Pardesi First turbaned
Sikh bus conductor driver in Manchester

Mukhtiar Singh Pardesi, the eldest son of Sikh high priest Mehar Singh Pardesi, was born in July 1938 in the village of Glotian, now in Pakistan. After the partition of 1947, the family moved to Patiala, Punjab, and later to the village of Garhi in the district of Udhampur, Jammu and Kashmir, to live with their grandparents. Mukhtiar received his education in the village school and went on to attend a higher secondary school in Udhampur, where he graduated with a matriculation degree in shorthand, science, geography, and maths. He was an expert in Hindi, Urdu, and Punjabi languages. In 1959, his mother and younger brother migrated to England, leaving him to look after his ageing grandfather. While doing that, he also attended school and tilled the family land, taking care of the seasonal crops. Mukhtiar Singh gained his first-class honours degree in 1962. Soon after his graduation, his grandfather Pandit Nanak Singh passed away. With his grandfather's demise, it left Mukhtiar alone at the time of harvest. But he was determined not to let his hard work of tilling the fields go to waste; he harvested the wheat crop, and soon after his father made arrangements for him to migrate to the UK.

The voucher system was introduced by the British Conservative government in 1962 for people from Commonwealth countries. Before the act was passed, citizens of Commonwealth countries had extensive rights to migrate to the UK. In response to a perceived heavy influx of immigrants, the conservative party government tightened the regulations, permitting only those with government-issued employment vouchers, thus limiting the numbers into the UK.

Mukhtiar Singh's father was already in the UK and was the first Sikh high priest of the Gurdwara Sahib in Manchester. Besides being a priest, he also worked in a firm owned by J. Chadwick & Sons based in Collyhurst, Manchester. Through this firm, he was able to access a working voucher for his son, and he was able to migrate to England in 1964 and join his family in Moss Side.

Arriving in England at the age of twenty-five years, being a well-educated and cultured young man, he became the general secretary of the Sikh Temple Guru Nanak Nirankari Gurdwara managed by the Sewak Jatha of Manchester Monton Street Moss Side Manchester. Though being the general secretary, he started his working career in Oldham Maple Mill in 1964 and later in Asia mill. Employed as a ring spinner, after working for some time in the cotton mill, by the end of the year 1964, he was engaged and married in June 1965 to a local Sikh girl, the daughter of a shop owner.

Mukhtiar Singh Pardesi worked in a cotton mill for two years until 1967 when he got the opportunity to become the first turbaned Sikh bus conductor employed by the Manchester Corporation Transport Committee (MCTD). He started his training on February 7, 1967, at the Hyde Road Bus Depot training school, and after two weeks of extensive training, he began his official duty on February 21, 1967. Gyani Sundar Singh Sagar, Mukhtiar's uncle, fought a seven-year-long battle with the MCTD and the Transport Workers Union (TGWU) to allow Sikhs with turbans to be employed as bus conductors and drivers.

Gyani Sundar Singh Sagar presented a large dossier referencing the two world wars in which Sikhs were under the British Raj (British Indian Army) to the committee with the support of all the Sikh community of Manchester and surrounding areas. With support from the local councillors and soldiers who had served in the British army in India and admired the Sikhs and especially the soldiers who had fought alongside the Sikh battalions, the city council and the union swayed their decision to let Sikhs be employed as platform staff on buses.

The media had shown deep interest in the case from the start, followed the case throughout and when the victory arose, they published a headline story on the front pages of the newspapers with a photo of Mr. Singh going about his duty as the first turbaned bus conductor in Manchester. The headline read:

> *The New Boy on Route 93 ... Mr Singh, Manchester's first turbanned conductor: It was the first day in a new job yesterday for Mukhtiar Singh Pardesi – and his turban, for, as he jumped aboard a No. 93 bus at the start of the 6.30am – 1.30pm shift, he became Manchester's first turbanned bus conductor.*

Victory

In the past, city transport regulations required drivers and conductors to wear only official caps, which prevented Sikhs wearing turbans from being employed. However, after a seven-year-long battle with the Manchester Corporation Transport Department and the Transport Workers Union, the city council finally allowed Sikhs to be employed as platform staff on buses, including as bus conductors. On January 4th, 1967, the city council made the decision to allow Sikhs with turbans to be employed, and Mr. Singh began his training as a bus conductor at Hyde Road Bus Depot on February 7th, 1967. He received one week of training in the training school, followed by another week of training on the roads under the supervision of an experienced bus conductor. After two weeks of extensive training, Mr. Singh began his official duty as Manchester's first turbaned bus conductor on February 21st, 1967.

Sardar Gurbax Singh Aziz

Sr. Gurbax Singh Aziz

Sardar Gurbax Singh Aziz lived in Punjab with his family until the great divide of 1947, when it became a part of Pakistan under British Raj. Before the partition, he was a prominent member of the Sarab Hind Bhatra Union, which took care of community affairs, and he was a keen reader of Urdu and Panjabi languages.

During the partition, many people were displaced along religious lines, and Gurbax Singh and his family found a home in the city of Patiala, Punjab. However, finding work was very difficult in a new city, so he began working as a self-employed door-to-door salesman. Despite these challenges, he remained active in community affairs, taking part in the establishment of a Sikh Temple in Patiala in 1958 and being elected as its cashier.

In 1965, he migrated to England and lived in Moss Side, Manchester, with his elder sister for a short while before starting to work in a cotton mill in Salford. Soon after, he bought a house and called his family over to England. As a member of the Gurdwara, he became the vice president of Guru Nanak Nirankari Gurdwara Moss Side in 1966 and took on various other roles in the committee from 1970 to 1977. In 1970-1978, he also served as the Sikh priest of the Gurdwara Sahib.

Meanwhile, writing became his hobby, and he wrote articles for community magazines and served as a news reporter for Sangat Samachar,

Sikh Sandesh, Sangat Sandesh, and Sangat weekly magazines. He also researched and wrote biographies of many prominent individuals in the community. He published a book of poems dedicated to Bhatra Sangat and the Sikh religion, celebrating their achievements in the UK. He also published a book called "Your Rituals are Reasons for My Poverty," in which he questioned the relevance of many of the outdated rituals that are still practiced today, despite having no standing in the Sikh religion.

After the redevelopment of Moss Side area, his family moved to Old Trafford, and he transferred his Gurdwara membership to Whalley Range Sikh Temple on Upper Chorlton Road. When the Gurdwara Sahib needed the services of a Sikh priest, Sardar Gurbax Singh offered his services and became priest of the Gurdwara Sahib. He later worked as a freelance Granthi, offering his services to Sikh Temples in the North West, including Preston, Liverpool, and as far as Middlesbrough and Scotland. Throughout his life, Sardar Gurbax Singh Aziz remained a devout Amritdhari Gur-Sikh and a keen believer in his religion and faith, following in the footsteps of Guru Nanak's mission.

Some Prominent Sikh People

Makhan Singh Digpal

Sardar Makhan Singh Digpal (Chand) lived in London, and his marriage was the very first marriage of a Bhatra Sikh, which took place in London Gurdwara Sahib. The marriage ceremony was performed by none other than Gyani Sundar Singh Sagar at Campbell Road Gurdwara Sahib in London. Later, he moved to Preston, where he worked in a cotton mill, and from there, he moved to Manchester with his family. While residing in Manchester, he became a member of Whalley Range Gurdwara Sahib. Being a member, he desired to become a committee member, but he was refused due to him being clean-shaven. The membership requested that if he became a fully fledged Sikh, he would be given a post on the management committee. He promised the Sangat that he would do so and straight away went and got baptized and became an Amritdhari Sikh. The Sangat, in their appreciation, gave him the post of president of the Gurdwara Sahib.

Kimat Singh Komal Digwa

Sardar Kimat Singh Komal came to England with his family on a ship S. S. Multan from Bombay in 1948. After landing at Tilbury docks, they went and lived in Liverpool for some time. In later years, they moved to Manchester in 1961 and made it their permanent place of residence. In 1966, he desired to become a Gurdwara president, but he was not eligible for the post due to being clean-shaven. Nevertheless, he was given a Siropa of Turban and made a promise to become a fully fledged Sikh before he could be given the post of president. In 1967, he fulfilled his vow and was elected as the president. Since then, he has been a keen devotee Sikh and has served the community in many capacities.

Pritam Singh Heera

Sardar Pritam Singh Heera came to England in the late '70s with his family and lived in Moss Side for some time. Later, he moved to Irlam, where he and his children worked in the Irlam steel company. Being a devoted Sikh family, they regularly visited Gurdwara Sahib, where Sardar Pritam Singh Ji recited Kirtan (hymns) every Sunday. He became the Gurdwara Sahib's regular Jatha doing Kirtan. His dedication was such that he used to travel on a bus from Irlam to Manchester and then the town center to the Gurdwara Sahib early each Sunday.

Mewa Singh Sathi

Sardar Mewa Singh Sathi lived in the Moss Side area of Manchester with his family. He, too, was a devoted Sikh and a member of the Guru Gobind Singh Gurdwara Whalley Range, where he recited Kirtan on a regular basis on Sundays, along with his colleague Sardar Pritam Singh. His younger son, Gurmukh Singh, played Dholki, accompanying the Jatha each Sunday.

Parkash Singh Sathi

Parkash Singh Sathi, a former bus conductor/driver and clean-shaven Sikh, later became an Amritdhari Sikh. He has been in the service of the Gurdwara Sahib in many capacities and was one of the five Pyares who laid the foundation stone of the new building in

Parkash Singh Potiwal

Parkash Singh Potiwal, Son of founder member of the Hulme community Gurdwara Sahib, Sardar Mangal Singh Potiwal; Parkash Singh who studied computer science at Lancashire Polytechnic and worked as computer hardware engineer, for Manchester based company, at the same time he started his side business of printing Asian wedding cards, which became a well established business. After few years he decided to open his own IT company after leaving his regular employment. Since then has been a very active member of the Gurdwara Sahib taking part in various roles and duties of the institution.

Gurdwara Sahib regulars Tunda Singh Pritam, Balwant Singh Digwa, Fauja Singh Roudh, Daleep Singh Digwa. were four gentlemen who took part in reading the Guru Granth Sahib Sikh scripture, whenever the celebration took place in the Gurdwara Sahib.

Bhai Sohan Singh Shairy

Bhai Sohan Singh Shairy lived in Raghumajra a town near the city of Patiala Punjab. He was employed as the local priest of the Gurdwara Sahib. In 1988 he came to England sponsored by his son Jagtar Singh Shairy. At the time the local Gurdwara in Whalley Range were in search for Granthi for their Gurdwara Sahib, Bhai Sohan Singh being a professional in this capacity he was stated as the head Granthi of the Gurdwara Sahib until after few years of service he retired due to ill health.

Bhai Harvinder Singh and Ragi Jatha

Bhai Harvinder Singh and his brother Sukhwinder Singh, along with their brother-in-law Bhai Jagdeep Singh Ji, are professional practicing Ragi Jatha from India. They were invited by the Guru Gobind Singh Gurdwara Sahib for their professional services as practicing Ragi Jatha. They were formerly employees of SGPC Amritsar and are currently in service at the Gurdwara Sahib Dukhniwaran Sahib Patiala, their city of residence. Their services to the Gurdwara Sahib and the Sangat are phenomenal and well respected by the Sikh community. The Gurdwara Sangat was blessed with their presence when the inauguration of the new build Gurdwara Sahib took place on November 11th, 2011. Since then, they have been recalled for their services from time to time. Nowadays, they have their sibling, Sardar Sukhsagar Singh, as their understudy who himself is a student of history at Punjabi University Patiala. The Jatha is well respected by the Sikh community and is always appreciated for their services.

Sardar Sewa Singh Himat

An educated gentleman who educated himself to city and guild engineering, and worked in an engineering firm as lathe turner a fully-fledged Sikh gentleman who was well educated in India as well as England and was a prominent member and general secretary of Guru Nanak Nirankari Gurdwara Moss Side, he dedicated his Servies just like his father Sardar Tirath Singh ji

Sardar Shingar Singh Sangi

Founder member of the Cheetham hill gurdwara he was the only person who had a printing press which he used to print Punjabi literature and wedding cards. He was well known throughout the Sikh community and a senior member of the Cheetham hill group.

Sardar Singh Bhaker

A member of the Cheetham hill group and participated in the reading of the Guru Granth Sahib during festivals and regularly priestly duties whenever required. His occupation was that he worked in ward and goldstone factory, manufacturing industrial electronic wire.

Charanjit Singh Potiwal

A dear colleague of sardar Singh Bhaker who also worked in Ward &Goldstone factory based on Fredrick Road Salford. A prominent senior member of the Cheetham hill group.

Ram Singh Sharma

Member of the moss side gurdwara who regularly participated in recitation of Kirtan (hymn singing) on Sundays with head priest playing cymbals.

Kartar Singh Digwa

A very tall gentleman member of the moss side gurdwara and an expert Dholki Player who used to accompany the priest every Sunday performing the Kirtan services in the gurdwara.

Conclusion

Having lived in Manchester since I came to England, in the Moss Side area full of different communities, cultures, and religions, an area which had a church, a synagogue, and a Sikh Temple of which my father Sardar Mehar Singh Pardesi was the high priest of the Gurdwara Sahib. In Monton Street, this area was thriving with diversity during the 60s/70s, an area full of harmony where people would go out of their way to help each other no matter what their ethnic background was or is.

Having lived amongst many different communities over the years, I have realized that there is very little history of Sikhs in Manchester who came to the city and worked tirelessly to make it their home. To achieve so much and through facing all kinds of rules and regulations that were being changed every so often by the then conservative government to control immigration into the UK, even though the country faced a shortage of manpower due to the loss of military forces in both world wars.

But there came a time when a Conservative member of parliament (MP) by the name of Enoch Powell delivered a speech to the conservative political center in Birmingham, United Kingdom "Rivers of Blood" in 1968. His speech strongly criticized mass immigration, especially from commonwealth countries. This brought in the Race relations Bill in controlling the migration to the UK. The backlash of that was the repercussions suffered by the Windrush migrants from Jamaica and West Indies, yet they were all British citizens. The Asian contingent also faced a similar situation but somewhat in a different context, especially the Sikhs who came here with their full-grown beards and turbans and of course different religious beliefs.

The host who had never been abroad except for the forces had never seen anyone like them before. Therefore they were entirely and utterly aliens for the English people. Each day they were called various names and taunted in the streets by youngsters being called towel heads and so on so forth. Moreover, they faced discrimination in getting employed in any decent factories. These occurred every day. But with resilience, we the Sikhs and the other communities came out on top by staying resilient and steadfast in our beliefs and faith in keeping our identity intact and never at any point lost our dignity through the hardships migrants faced.

I could document many more goings-on in the 60s and 80s; nevertheless, it makes me proud to have lived among so many different communities and people of different faiths, from whom I have learned so much from. All I have documented are my opinions with which I have lived the last seven/eight decades in the city of Manchester. Although there was very little past history documented, and what there is does not mention any achievements or does it provide who, where, what did, and how they did it?

This short history is about that, people who came, what they did, how they achieved, and above all what they went through to achieve it. Today we stand at a threshold of a fast-changing world of technology, and with that, we still need to carry on the good work which our elders built the foundation for us.

If we want to save our posterity and progeny from this dreaded and fast onslaught on our morals, religious, social, and cultural values, we should realize that there is no time to waste. We need to gird up our loins and accept the challenges which are denuding us and eroding everything good about our religion and culture, which distinguishes us from crude modern ways. Religion can play a very effective role in changing the worst scenario if applied cautiously, diligently, and judiciously. As far as us Sikhs are concerned, we have a sound heritage and a very modern and scientifically tested practical religion.

We need to come forward and teach our youngsters about the high values of our religion and the proud heritage we have inherited from our elders. Community leaders should educate our upcoming generation in the right ways. Although we are seeing drastic changes in orthodoxy which is good, the English language has become a phenomenon for them. In my opinion, this will lead to the loss of our mother language of Gurmukhi, which is essential for every Sikh family to teach their siblings. Our aim should be to enhance the changes and implement them in our homes to enable children to speak and read Gurmukhi so that our generation can move forward.

Regarding some of the rituals which are now predominant in our culture, most of which we do not know the real meaning, we still continue to practice them. On one hand, we say that we are Sikhs, but when it comes to our rituals, we practice centuries-old Brahmnical rituals that have no standing in the Sikh faith. As we are now in the twenty-first century, it is time to make up our minds which way we want to go. Because in time to come, today's generation will not be able to adhere to these old cultural rituals, and financial constraints are now prevailing on the public. We need to understand that our young generation today is educated and academic. Therefore, we need to move forward rather than practice meaningless rituals. This issue needs to be addressed by the community faith leaders.

Although there are quite a lot of names mentioned in the book, the reader and the descendants of the people mentioned should feel proud of their elders who faced many hurdles to give us what we have today. We need to carry the torch forward in the hope that one day we will also be old and remembered by someone in history.

This present work is a humble attempt at best and has been drawn mostly from my memory. Therefore, many gaps may appear in it, and there is no pretension of being a historian. To err is human, and readers are always magnanimous to forgive lapses in this sort of immature logic or inadequate vocabulary. Thanks, Sarup Singh Landa Manchester UK 2022

Bibliography

Encyclopaedia of Sikh religion. Nabha, B. K. (1930). Sudarshan Press Amritsar, Published Punjabi language department Patiala.

Guru Granth Sahib. (n.d.). From the mouth of the first Mehl Saveeae Mehalae Pehile Kae. (p. 1389).

Encyclopaedia of Sikh religion and culture. Dogra, R. C., & Mansukhani, G. S. (1995). Vikas Printing.

Bhat- Vahis. (n.d.). Record and dairies maintained by Bhat- priests of their clients. Panjabi University Patiala Archives.

Bhai Bannu. (n.d.). A Volume by Bhai Bannu.

Rose, H. A. (1924). Glossary of Tribes and Casts of the Punjab.

Guru Granth Sahib. (n.d.). Sawaiys from the Mouth of the great fifth Mehl, Hymns in praise of Guru Ram Das Ji. (p. 1385).

Castle, R. C., & Weller, P. (1993). Religions in the UK. Published by University of Derby in Association with interfaith network for UK.

Shaad, G. R. S. (n.d.). Krantik Lehra (revolutionary wave) (p. 15).

Shaad, G. R. S. (1951). Ibid. Punjabi Press India.

Religions in the UK Multi-faith directory. (n.d.). Published by Derby University in association with the Interfaith Network for the United Kingdom.

McAuliffe, M. A. (n.d.). The Sikh Religion.

Aziz, G. S. G. (n.d.). From the files of Sardar Gurbax Singh Aziz.

Glossary

Amrit – a ceremony of initiation of Sikh Baptisment into Sikh religion, introduced by Guru Gobind Singh when he founded the Khalsa in 1699

Amrit Dhari – a baptised Sikh who has taken Khande-di-Pahul and become a Khalsa and dons the five K's

Azad – Independent self governing

Bhai - An epithet of respect prefixed to name of a Gentlemen

Bhatra – Name of a caste or tribe in Punjab India

Dharamsala – Inn, house for pilgrims, alms house a place for travellers,

Gurbani – holy words spoken by the Guru's (Sikh hymns)

Giani – Sage, Scholar, philosopher, learned,

Granthi – Sikh scripture reader/ priest or efficient

Gurdwara – place of Sikhs worship, God's house place for pilgrims, devotees, disciples

Jalliwala-Bagh - a memorial park, a museum dedicated to Udham Singh Azad, located near the Golden Temple complex Amritsar preserved in memory of the innocent people massacred on the orders of Michael O'Dwyer in 1919

Jatha – Group of three learned hymn singers in Sikh Temple

Jathedar – a person chosen head a body of Sikhs to ensure discipline also central head of Sikhs worldwide.

Khalsa – Name of a baptised Sikhs who has taken Amrit

Kirat – work; living by one's honest labour basic beliefs of a Sikh

Kirtan – Devotional worship, praises of God. Sikh Gurus composed hymns and sang them, using classical "Ragas"

Kaur – name given to Sikh women

Nagar – Village or a town

Nam – literally means the Holy Name, also it stands for supreme reality

Padh –Recital of sacred text, prayer

Padhi – Reader, reciter of scared text

Pangat - Line or a Row in Gurdwara dining hall an institution of equality between rich and poor, cast and creed, institute started by the third Guru Amar Das Ji.

Sangat – Religious congregation, company, Association

Sangladeep –Sri Lanka, an independent country in South Asia and lies in the Indian Ocean in Bay of Bengal

Simran – to remember, meditate upon God's name, Prayer

Sikh – a person who believes in the ten Gurus and Guru Granth Sahib holy scriptures of the Sikh religion

Sr – Sardar Sikh gentleman same as Mr.

Singh – Sikh men take on the surname of Singh after initiation into the Khalsa fold on their Baptism into they take on the name of "Khalsa brotherhood "Amrit"